# CAR BOMBS TO COOKIE TABLES

## THE YOUNGSTOWN ANTHOLOGY

Edited by Jacqueline Marino and Will Miller

© by Belt Publishing

All rights reserved
Printed in the United States of America
2016

ISBN-10: 0985944188
ISBN-13: 978-0-9859441-8-6

Belt Publishing
1667 E. 40th Street #1G1
Cleveland, Ohio 44120
www.beltmag.com

Book design by Leah Perrino
Cover design by Leah Perrino
Cover photo: Inside Youngstown Sheet & Tube
30 years after it closed. *Sean Posey*

To our families

# CONTENTS

# WORK

# RISE

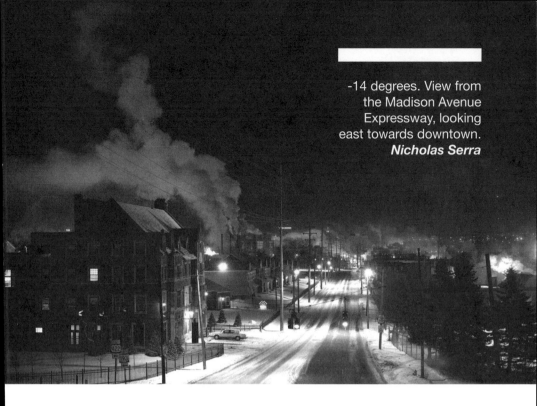

# SINKIN' DOWN IN YOUNGSTOWN:
## AN INTRODUCTION

**D**ale Maharidge and Michael Williamson began reporting *Journey to Nowhere*, their 1985 work on the new American underclass, in Youngstown, by exploring the ruins with ex-steelworkers, chronicling their hopelessness and despair.

With that book, Maharidge and Williamson declared Youngstown dead. Industry built the city, and industry buried it. This became Youngstown's dominant narrative. It begins in iron and steel and ends in flames and decay, sometimes with a subplot driven by violent mobsters and corrupt politicians.

Over the past four decades, however, this story has not been told by residents as much as it has been told to them. The people of Youngstown continued to live in and near the city, to work as well as they could. They raised their children to become not just survivors but competitors. In many cases, they raised their children to leave Youngstown, and their children left as well as they knew how. But there is something magnetic about Youngstown to those of us who once lived there, an invisible pull that is as hard to describe as it is for outsiders to believe.

In these pages, we try.

Don't be fooled by the cover; this book is not about Youngstown's industrial past.

Don't be fooled by the title; this book is not about Youngstown crime or nostalgia.

This is a book about Youngstown experiences, told by the people who lived them.

Not all of Youngtown's diverse communities are sufficiently represented in the book. We wish we had received more submissions from Asian, African-American, and Hispanic writers. The ethnic diversity of our writers mirrors that of the Youngstown population around 1920: English, Irish, Eastern European, and Southern European names fill the Table of Contents. Our 45 contributors span seven decades in age. Some shout and some whisper. Some make you want to devour an Alberini's pepperoni roll. There is no definitive Youngstown experience expressed here because there is no definitive Youngstown experience. There are only experiences: love, hardship, hang-ups, defeat, joy, kindness, devotion—you will find all of these and more. This is a book about life as it was, is, and will be lived in the Mahoning Valley.

Bookstores should not be stocking this title in the True Crime section. While several contributors reference Youngstown's much-discussed mob history, there are no mob stories here. Our title encompasses the best and the worst representations of our city. The car bomb, once called a "Youngstown tune-up," is the worst. It was the execution method of choice by mobsters here at one time. It became obsolete when they did. The cookie table, as discussed by author Nikki Trautman Baszynski, is one of the best. The tradition began at the weddings of families too poor to buy wedding cakes. The guests brought cookies instead. This tradition still exists, though Youngstown bakeries often provide the cookies now (as well as scrumptious wedding cakes).

We have an abundance of essays by contributors who have made rebuilding the city's narrative their personal or professional missions, but this isn't a work of boosterism. In fact, you may get angry reading it. In the Mahoning Valley, memory is "a significant source of conflict," according to Sherry Lee Linkon and John Russo in *Steeltown U.S.A.: Work & Memory in Youngstown*, a must-read for anyone who wants to understand the city. Since the 1800s, residents have been both proud of their area's past industrial prominence and consumed with establishing their place within it. Collectively proud of their city but ethnically, racially, and socioeconomically divided, Youngstown residents fought those in power and sometimes one another. As Linkon and Russo remind us, workers were often segregated in the mills. In the 1910s and '20s, for instance, the Irish worked in transportation, the Italians in masonry, and Hungarians and Slovaks in the open hearth. African-Americans worked general labor, often in the dirtiest jobs in the plant. Native-born Americans were supervisors. This ethnic and class segregation existed in the neighborhoods as well, resulting in nothing like a community.

But decades have passed since the mills closed. Through words and images expressed honestly and fearlessly, we find healing—and meaning. This book will do more than relay stories; it will help those of us who consider ourselves part of Youngstown nation understand our past, so we can move thoughtfully into our futures. We also hope to make you smile. (See the original story by Youngstown's favorite actor, Ed O'Neill.)

Some of our authors are national figures, such as short story writer and novelist Christopher Barzak and the Rust Belt poet Rochelle Hurt. Others are publishing their debut works in this volume. Some stories are told in narrative form, others in verse, essay, illustration, or documentary photography. All are loosely grouped by themes: Loss, Family, Work, Rise. You will find snapshots and musings, profiles and history. Again, this is not a book of nostalgia, nor is it a manifesto or a lament. It is a confrontation.

Maharidge and Williamson said they chose Youngstown for their

study of the struggles of the 1980s underclass because it typified
"the agony of dozens of American cities"—but Youngtown does not
exist to be "typical." Youngstown can teach. It can transcend. This
book is for the people of Youngstown, past, present, and future; for
their parents and their parents' parents, for their children and their
children's children, but mostly it is for themselves. It is an examination of memory and conscience, sometimes a celebration, always
a mirror. From hard hats to cookie tables, black lungs to football
glory, the Valley of our past is in these pages. *My sweet Jenny, we're
sinkin' down*. It is the only way through.


*Jacqueline Marino*
Kent, Ohio


*Will Miller*
St. Augustine, Florida

# LOSS

Wreckage inside the abandoned (now demolished) Paramount Theatre.
*Leah Perrino*

# "DO WE HAVE ANY ROCK AND ROLLERS OUT THERE TONIGHT?"

is the first question     the singer swinging it
like blood through the lion's mouth
      adjusting his crotch through
            fishnet     his day job

regulation autoworker     the microphone
up against his tongue     the crowd
      drunk in the downtown
            of '79     my father     everyone

considering what they are out there     tonight each Saturday night
coming down West Federal
      stoned dumb on Youngstown Brown
            dumb sweet on downtown traffic

past old theaters queued     for demolition     grand balconies
segregating
      generations     of questions
            to which the speaker adds another

then ignites it in a fit     of midnight arson     belts it
with bouquets     of beer and time cards
      does it while the room's is still
            a room     before the question's spoiled

rotten     he wants an answer
because he's aware of the terrible
      acoustics     of his city and the noise
            he needs to make     he needs to.

*Allison Davis*

# ANOTHER MAN'S TRASH

*By Sarah Stankorb*

"Jump!" someone yelled, in the wild, certain tone of a kid who's hatched a plan.

"Yeah, now!" Another schemer bellowed.

Our neighbor Ben had climbed the tree above our Kool-Aid stand. He was perched, eyes manic, feet and hands hooked onto various branches, mentally preparing to hurl himself into the path of oncoming traffic. He was our velociraptor, our jackal.

Ben's eyes darted to the street, the car cruising up fast, and he froze. Our frantic voices raised in rapid succession:

"Kool-AID!"

"STOP!"

"GET SOME KOOOOL-AID!"

"Come on man, stop the—"

The car whooshed by without pause.

"Shit."

Ben shimmied down the tree.

"You wuss. They got away."

There was some cussing, slights to Ben's masculinity. How were we supposed to stop traffic without him leaping in front of it, feigning injuries that could be made to go away with a simple purchase?

"You jump out of the tree next time!" he countered, and, with no volunteers, we glumly sat back down at the curb.

On any given day there were six to nine of us, depending upon tagalong little siblings and whose weekend it was for custody visits. Along with G.I. Joe, He-Man, and Jem, we had each other.

The bar down past the corner, Spanky's, wouldn't open for a few hours and the sort that frequented it wouldn't drop ten cents on our line of beverages anyway. No, the drunks only came up our street at night, pounding on the door, demanding to use the phone, sometimes thinking they lived there.

This had been the first car in what felt like hours. It always felt like hours, waiting, while we sold Kool-Aid, while we ran yard sales and haggled over one another's toys. I bought my first Barbie that way, a sticky thing with a glob of gum in her hair that my neighbor Jessie sold me for a dime. I gave it a haircut. She demanded it back, so I hid it in my sock drawer.

"Now what?"

"We wait."

It was the sort of neighborhood where most of our parents were in and out of work, but enough bills got paid that we all generally stayed put. Our little side street ran off Trumbull Avenue in Girard, near 422, right at the border with Youngstown—the place where, you know, we were told, people got killed.

We were a bunch of poor, white kids but didn't know enough to know we were poor and didn't know enough people outside our neighborhood to think much about being white. It would be years before I'd hear the term "white trash" and wonder why people thought it so especially offensive that white people might be poor. Was it acceptable for other people to be poor? Were we disposable?

On good days we'd hear the happy scrape of a lawnmower or wagon trucking down the street, its driver, Otis, at the helm. After a period of concern over being pulled over, he'd acquired a few miniature license plates for his fleet of "cars." Atop the mowers, he bungeed down a milk crate where he kept his treasures—kids' treats to distribute and crunched-up pop cans, other people's trash.

"Otis is mentally handicapped," my mother told me once or twice. "I don't know if he really thinks those are cars or not, but don't argue with him about it. You'll hurt his feelings." And out she sent me to play with him.

Otis was a rambler, a steel-city Pied Piper, beckoning children with the clatter of his cars filled with pop cans and offering us quarters, stickers, and sometimes candy. It wasn't an exchange of goods but gift giving. He collected things other people considered trash—scrap metal we gave him—and gave us treasures. It wasn't commerce.

His circuit surely spanned all of Parkwood, maybe swept over the border into Youngstown. We didn't know where Otis lived or even if he lived in a proper house, but he certainly had a garage for all the red-blue-green-rust colored mowers. Maybe he drove those mowers over people's yards for money. I don't know.

"Otis!" one or nine of us would cry and hustle over to his car of the day. If someone had gathered pop cans, they would turn them over, but the smallest among us just appeared at his side.

"Out driving my car," Otis started. We'd nod. Of course he was. He was an adult. He was much taller than us. I was never sure how old, 18, maybe 30, but definitely not as old as our parents. But he was a grown-up, the nicest grown-up we knew.

Otis showed off his license plate. We'd seen it before, but it didn't matter. It was a colorful thing, hung on with wire or large twist-ties. He loved it and his cars, took pride in them.

It wasn't that he drove unconventional vehicles, that he was a tall black man who attracted broods of little white kids; no, it was that pride that made him so anomalous. He loved his cars in a way that our parents didn't love their things. They maintained houses, yards, rusting automobiles with mufflers hung on with coat hangers, but those things didn't stir their emotions.

"Wow," we all breathed in a chorus over the license plate.

Every once in a while, Otis would appear with these very official-looking stickers, white letters on a black background, the sort you might use to number your mailbox. Whether you'd brought him pop cans or not, Otis had something to give you.

I waited until most everyone else had gotten a letter and shyly asked for an S. He presented it, and I was struck by the notion that I had no idea where to put something so precious. It stood for me—Sarah. Some of the other kids stuck their stickers on their bikes. My parents had already sold mine.

For a long time, I left that sticker flipped over in my room, un-stuck, until its adhesive wore off, and it became just a useless scrap.

Days winded together as they do in childhood: ball games in the big field behind our house, one owned by the electric company, with a transformer off to one side. To the other direction lived an impossibly old woman whose somehow more ancient son-in-law—a snappish geezer with bad eyes and worse teeth—had put up an electric fence to help her deter children and their stray balls. It didn't work (my brother tested it by sending me under). It wasn't a place that wanted kids.

So if not gathered round Otis, playing ball or haggling for cash, we climbed and warred in the ditch behind our field. It was a swampy borderland out of earshot from our parents and so far back that it abutted a baseball field frequented by another band of dirt-smudged kids. Their street connected to ours along a long bend, and from the ditch you could hear Otis coming. I don't know if he ever stopped for those kids, but by the time we made it out over the field and onto Earl Street, he was there for us. He was ours.

"It's a beautiful day," he'd announce, and it was. Otis grinned. We grinned, happily filthy, peering into his treasure keeper milk crate.

"Candy!" We became a mass of elbow-thrusting, shoving joy. And Otis laughed and gave it away—not the penny stuff either. Candy that cost a nickel apiece, easily.

"Do you have any cans?"

A few of us shrugged. I felt bad, like I'd let him down.

"Just keep looking. Keep looking. You'll find them." We promised we'd look. Someone said they'd seen one in the ditch. We could go retrieve it.

All through the start of school, through the age when I was big enough to cross streets and walk up to Lamancusa's for penny candy with the other kids, Otis was there. Out less frequently in the cold months (and who would want to walk a car in the snow?), but there. A presence, an ambling, rattling bearer of quarters and candy. A collector of things people littered and a gatherer of kids left to scatter.

The summer before third grade, I was old enough to know we were moving but not really understand why. I heard the term bankruptcy without capturing its meaning. Our house would soon not be ours, and the old lady's white-haired, bad-breathed son-in-law was taking our house. He even had the nerve, after taking his bent and creaky time painting the back of our garage to scream at us for kicking balls at it. It was a marvel, watching so much air gust through such aged and evil lungs.

"He's such a bastard," Ben muttered under his breath. Bastard. Yes, that word sounded right. That old man was a complete bastard.

We lagged in moving out because there was nowhere to move to. What could be sold was sold, what could be delayed was delayed, until a week or two before we were to be forced out, my father found a rental that had been so trashed by its previous tenants that the landlord would let us live there in exchange for my dad's labor fixing it.

It was still in Girard, but it was way down 422, past the place my mother always reminded me there had once been signs marking the point at which blacks should stay out. Despite her perpetual civil rights lessons, I had only ever wondered whether the old-timey racists had made the signs themselves or had them printed up like street signs. But now I wondered how long ago that was, whether all those people were for sure dead now.

I don't know if I cried when we moved. I'm pretty sure I didn't say goodbye to Otis. It would have been like saying goodbye to Santa Claus, a figure too impressive to need a change-of-address notice. But once we got to the new house, I certainly cried. My father painted my bedroom a cotton-candy pink and painted over the bull's-eye on the door, filled in what looked like bullet holes. My mother shoved me out the front door to play, but there were no kids in our neighborhood. The air was clear and silent. No balls bouncing. No roving pack of heckles and cheery jeers. No scrape of Otis's cars. I never knew where all he walked, but I now knew where he didn't go. A bitter old man had my house, would by now have chased the kids out of our yard for good. And I had this, a decaying street on the far side of town, without promise of more—stickers, candy, traveling treasure—coming around the bend.

# THE B&O, CROSSROADS OF TIME AND SPACE

*By Christopher Barzak*

When the writer Henry Miller stepped down from the train he'd taken to Youngstown, OH, in 1940, he saw two girls, heads wrapped in scarves, picking their way down the bluff of a hillside by the railroad, and thought of his days traveling through Greece, the heat and dust and flies, the Greek peasant women, baskets carried on their heads, slowly descending on bare feet. He remarked that this first vision of Youngstown was where the resemblance to Greece began and ended.

A line of factories and mills stretched from east to west along the railroad and the Mahoning River, sending torrents of flame and black clouds of smoke into the canopy of the valley sky above him. Not even Dante, said Miller to a friend, had imagined such an inferno. From Pittsburgh to Youngstown he had ridden, surrounded by fire and smoke, and nothing but cars, cars, cars sitting in the fenced-in parking lots of the mills, those shining chariots of independence, their owners breaking their backs inside the factories, in the most stultifying kind of work Miller could imagine in order to own one.

The railroad line Henry Miller came in on is no longer a passenger service. Instead the B&O Station sits atop the hillside where Miller stood watching two peasant girls as they made their way down to a neighborhood at the bottom of a smoke-filled hollow, and trains go by, squealing, horns blaring as they disappear into the distance of east or west. It is not a stop for anyone; it is a point of no departure. A person can stand on that platform waiting for someone to arrive, or waiting to leave, and never move again.

No flames lick the skies here any longer; no smoke fills the hollows of the valley where 20 different languages once choked the air. The factories have been demolished or have collapsed or sit rusting, waiting for someone to return to them. Those peasant girls? Their neighborhood no longer exists. It is a grassy bowl beneath blue skies and a crayon sun.

If you turn your eye to the side, though, and look through the perforation that Henry Miller made in time, you can see the beautiful wreckage of another city, one that sits side by side with the one that spreads out before you.  It is like seeing ghosts, this work I favor. You must be willing to see one before it will reveal itself. You must believe in its possibility before it can be real. Henry Miller saw it on an afternoon in 1940, and so I see it, a mote that floats in my eye beside whatever I'm looking at, wherever I turn my gaze.

When I step down from the platform at the B&O Station, I see the defunct rails, the murk of the Mahoning River running alongside, but I also see two girls, heads wrapped in scarves, picking their way down the hill to their neighborhood. The houses down there sit in clouds of smoke and dusty resignation. Turkeys and chickens peck at the ground of backyards.

Their mothers stand on square front lawns, wringing their hands in their aprons, waving to the girls as they approach.

These girls, they are their mother's dreams, they are knots in a rope to the future, which the mothers climb across, hand over hand, like sturdy athletes, until they see a man from the future looking through Henry Miller's spy hole, and then the empty hillside behind him, the abandoned tracks of the B&O. It is then and there that the mothers pause in their crossing of time and space.

They hang, these mothers, suspended like grapes, wincing in the sunlight. Nothing they thought would be in their futures looks how they had imagined. As Henry Miller observed between Youngstown and the island of Crete, the similarities of the past and the future begin and end with these girls, their girls, those peasant girls descending a hillside in 1940, with scarves wrapped over their heads.

Myself? As Plato describes the human form moving through time, my back is to the future, the wind blowing my hair forward in waves toward the past. I dare not look over my shoulder.

*"The B&O: Crossroads of Time and Space" was first published in Muse, December 2010.*

# THE LONG WAY HOME

*by Christine McBurney*

Facebook only allows you to list one hometown on your profile, but I have two. I was born in Brooklyn Heights. Not Ohio. New York. Just across the East River from lower Manhattan. But I spent the better part of my formative years in Strudders (Struthers). Not New York. Ohio. Just across the Mahoning River from the Yunkstown (Youngstown) Sheet & Tube mills.

Growing up I'd spend holidays and summers in New York City and the rest of my childhood in Struthers. My classmates detected that I was from somewhere else, and my New York summer friends did too. I don't have a New York accent, or the Pittsburghese accent that so many folks in Youngstown have. Rather, I have the enviable in-between, non-regional accent that radio and TV people and actors pay good money to perfect. But being from two places is like not really being from either.

So I entered Brooklyn Heights, NY, as my hometown on Facebook.

I've come to realize that I've spent most of my adult life trying to erase my memories of growing up in Mahoning County. I always pincd for New York. Living in Struthers felt like a punishment. I pined for my mother, a Youngstown native who insisted she needed to live in New York because there was no work in Youngstown. When trying to raise my sister and me in 1960s Brooklyn became impossible, we were sent to live with her parents in Youngstown. You know your town is bad when it makes your own mother leave. She shipped us by train just before I began kindergarten. Grandpa worked on the Pittsburgh & Lake Erie Railroad, so he probably got a discount on the fares, and grandma was a homemaker just a year older than I am now, always resplendent in housecoat and curlers. Today, fifty is the new thirty. Back then, fifty was seventy. It would be the first of many train trips back and forth between New York and

Struthers.

It wasn't Youngtown's fault that our mom couldn't find a job, or that there wasn't much for teenagers in the '70s to do except drink, cruise, and spend weekends at the Boardman Rollercade. I loved my mother's stories (always in black and white in my imagination) about the 1950s and '60s in Youngstown—stories of sock hops at the ethnic halls and going downtown in hats and gloves to picture shows. Why couldn't we have that? Why did we get a looming recession instead?

At least there was the fabulous Idora Park, an old-school, better version of Geauga Lake, complete with a ballroom, train, and a grand carousel. I remember feeling sad when I realized sometime during high school that I was getting too old to ride my favorite white pony. Today's hipsters would probably find riding a carousel ironic and retro. These words were not in my 16-year-old vocabulary.

Whenever I dig out old photo albums, I see the duality of my two hometowns in two professional photographs of 5-year-old me in my same favorite red dress with white lace collar. In the photo my mother had taken in Brooklyn, my long hair is thick and shiny. I look like a mini-Breck Girl. The light is amber and gauzy, my chubby hand placed coyly under my chin. As the family story goes, this photo hung in the window as an advertisement in a photographer's shop. Flash-forward a year or so to the second photo, the one that my grandmother had taken in downtown Youngstown, maybe at McCrory's or Strauss's. I'm in the same dress, but my long hair, now stringy, is in a sloppy ponytail, having clearly lost some of its luster to my proximity to industrial pollution and my grandfather's chain-smoking Winstons—a toxic combination that I'm sure contributed to my adult-onset asthma. My chubby hands are placed in my lap. I'm still smiling and happy-looking, but the lighting is harsh, the earlier glamour having disappeared in the smoke and haze of the mills.

We only lived in Youngstown for a year before my grandparents moved next door to the city of Struthers where I remember my grandfather paying $7,000 cash for half of a duplex that had originally been built for its workers by the Youngstown Sheet & Tube Company. I know now that YS & T built my humble, hollow, tile-blocked duplex in an effort to provide better benefits to its employees after bloody strikes, near-government seizure, and abysmal worker living conditions. It was a kind of corporate welfare; company houses in Struthers, Campbell, and Youngstown that were an easy walk to the South Gate, General Works Office, Coke Plant, and Rod and Wire Departments. "Overlook Plat" was the official name of the last development of 54 units built and it was originally rented to American-born workers, particularly those of British or German ancestry. By 1970, when we moved in, these houses were already being rented and sold to people unaffiliated with YS&T. A big selling point was that it was an easy walk to the P&LE Railroad for my grandpa, too, and now that I think of it, a move to put my sister and me in a better (whiter) school district.

One of my fondest memories of Struthers centers around my grandpa, who, when grandma needed a break—a trip to the beauty parlor—would drag me along to the Sons of Italy Club. I can still see its round art deco mirrors and dim interior. Cigarette in mouth, grandpa would hoist me up onto bar stools and order me a Shirley Temple. His mill and railroad buddies would teasingly call me Gina Lollobrigida and give me a nickel for the bowling machine. I had never seen onc of the Italian actress's films, but I thought her name sounded like music and I liked to bowl, so I indulged them.

Visits to the Youngstown area today are rare. My mother and the grandparents who reared me are buried there, and I'm ashamed to say I rarely visit their graves. My only living relatives in Ohio, the Boardman cousins, have since moved further out into exurbia when that suburb (so I heard) started to get a little bluer around the collar.

Growing up, the term "Rust Belt" was just on the verge of entering the lexicon. Our community began to erode on September 19, 1977, or "Black Monday," when YS&T announced it would close the Campbell Works. I was in middle school. There was talk about jobs being shipped overseas and families having to move. It's astounding how easily and how much teenagers are able to block out most of the world's workings. This was especially true before the internet and cable TV. All I knew was that I would no longer have to wipe the soot off my grandmother's windowsills. But then, I missed the six o'clock whistle. Before the mill closure, I knew what time it was because I had the whistle as my cue, a signal that I should probably start heading home for supper.

Even though I don't visit much anymore, something of the Youngstown area still sticks to me, like that soot on grandma's windowsill. People always ask me about the Mafia. Who did I know? What did I see? They assume, with my dark hair and outgoing personality, that I must be Italian. And perhaps connected. My family is not Italian, nor is it connected. I did grow up with so many classmates of Italian heritage that some of it must've rubbed off. Funnily enough, I had my DNA tested recently and despite my Northern European parents and grandparents, the results of the 23andme test kit show I am 40 percent Italian.

Actually, now that I think of it, Struthers does have a distinction to be proud of. Its high school launched the highest-powered student-run radio station in the country. I worked there all four years as a DJ, newscaster, and board engineer for the various ethnic "polka" hours (Croatian, Slovak, Ukrainian, etc.). During a typical radio lab class, I'd rip a story off the AP wire and anchor a newscast. One day, I read a story on the air about Ronald Carabbia, the man who was once believed to be the boss of organized crime in Youngstown and who had recently been sentenced to life in prison for his role in the 1977 murder of Irish mob boss and Clevelander Danny Greene. Naïve, teenage me ran from radio class to the journalism room, where I found a different Ronnie Carabbia, a hunky football player and a member of the Student Prints newspaper staff. The room was buzzing as usual with boys and girls, some focused on getting the news out, others on making it. I walked right up to Ronnie and asked if he was related to Ronald Carabbia, a guy whose name I'd just read on the air. The air went out of the room. Glances were exchanged. Everything stopped. The next thing I knew, Ronnie had taken a thick rubber band, wrapped it around his thumb, slowly pulled the other end towards him, shot it at me, and then left the room. I was bewildered. The other students quickly crowded around me. "He's gonna' put a hit out on you," someone said. "A what?" It was at that moment, in Mrs. Benton's 11th grade journalism class, that I received my education on the Youngstown mob.

I did go back to Struthers about a year ago. A friend was throwing a spaghetti dinner fundraiser at the high school for his son, who was about the same age as mine, and who would eventually succumb to cancer. I hadn't seen this friend since high school, but I felt like I needed to go. I went alone on a crisp fall day, early enough to do a little tour around the place. Many of the geographic and emotional touchstones were no longer there. The original building had been torn down and rebuilt. I am a high school teacher now, and I feel a twinge of envy when my former students who are visiting me see their old lockers. There no longer exists a locker with a code I know. No basketball hoop, under which I first kissed a boy. My junior high, elementary, and kindergarten buildings have also been demolished or rebuilt. The Newport movie theatre where I had my first date is gone. Bird Bath, the local swimming hole, is gone. Even the street curb at the corner of Garfield and Lincoln has been replaced. I couldn't believe the old "WPA 1939" stamp that I noticed every day walking to and from school for 12 years had been replaced by a boring, blank slab of concrete. Perhaps the most devastating losses are those backdrops of my adolescent weekends spent in search of boys from other schools at Idora Park and the Rollercade. The former burnt down and the latter is now a bakery. It's kind of hard to try to reconnect to a place when they bulldoze your memories.

This past summer, my two hometowns collided when my sister and I took our boys to New York. My son, also a frequent visitor to the Big Apple, wanted to show it off to his cousin, who'd never been there. My nephew had the usual list of tourist attractions he wanted to see: Times Square, the Statue of Liberty, Ground Zero.

For my sister and me, Brooklyn is ground zero. The first excursion was a train downtown and a walk across the Brooklyn Bridge to the old neighborhood whose streets are lined with 19th century brownstones, a far cry from the Sheet & Tube duplex where we were raised. I had recently seen a CBS Sunday Morning show about a woman who had bought and lovingly restored the old Idora Park merry-go-round. She had it installed in Brooklyn Bridge Park. I shared the YouTube video with my sister and she agreed that we had to find and ride it with our kids. We walked in a labyrinthine path beneath the bridge, getting lost a few times until we spied a giant glass box perched on the East River. Inside was the merry-go-round now called Jane's Carousel.

Here, in a park, facing lower Manhattan, was the carousel I had ridden throughout my childhood, summer after summer in Youngstown, the city to which I'd been banished from Brooklyn, in Brooklyn! We bought our tickets and waited for the smiling toddlers and their parents to disembark. I recognized my favorite white pony, the one I used to wait for until his saddle was empty. My sister and I were girls again, squealing with delight while our young men just rolled their eyes.

Riding up and down on my pony, being blasted by that loud, wild, baroque-like organ music, my eyes moved from the ceiling with its beautiful hand-painted idyllic scenes to the almost sinister, slanted mirrors. In my reflection, I saw the sad little girl stuck in Struthers, trying to get back to Brooklyn. And, at the same time, with each revolution of the carousel, I saw that same little girl on the Idora Park merry-go-round surrounded by Brooklyn Bridge Park, not the woods of Mill Creek Park. These split images blurred and overlapped, but they never really converged. Two hometowns. Two moms. Two halves of a duplex … there's no place like home …

What should have been a moment of identity integration became something like Dorothy's post-Oz haze. While my sister and I watched *The Wizard of Oz*, my sister teared up as Dorothy delivered those famous last lines, "There's no place like home, there's no place like home." I smirked, always detecting a slight sense of Dorothy's disappointment in getting what she wished for, as if the reason she repeated this phrase so many times was because she had to convince herself that it was true. Yeah, yeah, there is no place like home, but she'd just been to Oz! Don't you think that once she compared the pigsties of her Kansas farm to the yellow brick road, it wouldn't be too long before she was longing for Oz again? She had to make a choice. She chose home, but I never bought it. Now Facebook said I had to choose between Brooklyn and Struthers, between New York and Ohio, and I thought I did. But I couldn't. I couldn't choose the way Dorothy did. But what I could do was for the first time was emotionally connect to the place where I grew up. Not by revisiting Youngstown itself, but by riding the Idora Park carousel in Brooklyn. Ironic.

After that trip, I returned to my current home, Cleveland, which to me is part New York, part Youngstown. I came back with a new sense of curiosity and even pride and gratitude. As a 20-something roaming the streets of New York, I had no real sense of the role the Rust Belt played in history. And let me tell you, after witnessing the incremental Disneyfication of Times Square, I am more excited about the reurbanization of the Rust Belt than the suburbanization of New York.

I want to reconnect more to my Rust Belt roots. I know more about New York City than I do about Youngstown. And that needs to change. And it was going so well until the other day *Fortune Magazine* christened Cleveland the new Brooklyn. Youngstown has gotten some pretty good press lately too. What will they say next? "Youngstown is the new Queens?"

The Rust Belt isn't the East Coast. The Rust Belt built the East Coast. You know the party's over when the cute guy from another school finally asks the chubby local girl to dance. No thanks, *Fortune*, and, with all due respect to the place of my birth, no thanks, Brooklyn. I'm changing my hometown on Facebook to Cleveland Heights. There's no place like home.

# THE MYSTIQUE OF CEDARS LOUNGE

*By Elaine Arvan Andrews*

I first heard of Cedars in the late 1980s. While my high school boyfriend and I listened to Velvet Underground cassettes in his bedroom, he would brag about sneaking into Cedars to see punk bands. As we cruised by the old Gallagher Building on North Hazel at night with the windows down, I gawked at the punks smoking against the brick walls. I felt the muffled rhythms throbbing like a weird heartbeat in a skeletal downtown. My curiosity about Cedars lasted longer than that boyfriend. In the fall of 1990, I finally stepped through the smoke for my first encounter with underground Youngstown.

That night, I went to see the Februarys with some friends. Cedars was a dark, gritty, and fascinating place. As the band powered through a set, we squeezed through the crowd and found seats in a back booth. The music was too loud for us to talk. The long-haired boys slouched in their unbuttoned flannel shirts, and the girls, like me, wore dark lipstick and black-velvet chokers. I longed to be part of this scene.

At Cedars, I fell in love with the energy of live shows. And it was here that I experienced a fierce pride in my hometown, which, at the time, was well over a decade in fallout from Black Monday 1977. That infamous year overlaps with Cedars's beginnings in the late 1970s, when Tommy Simon talked his father into inviting college kids from Youngstown State University to play independent music. An old way of life had died, but Cedars Lounge and the punk rock movement were just beginning. For the next few decades, a vibrant independent music scene would develop around this former steelworkers' bar. Many national and international acts would play here en route to Cleveland: The Goo Goo Dolls, The Dead Milkmen, The Waitresses, Concrete Blonde, Jonathan Richman, Cracker, Wayne Kramer (from the legendary MC5), Gogol Bordello, Death of Samantha, King Missile, and, perhaps most famously, the Dead Boys.

The crowds at Cedars had a reputation for being large, enthusiastic, and often rowdy. In his autobiography, Cheetah Chrome
recalls playing there with the Dead Boys in 1986: "The place was jam
packed to the rafters; there were even people sitting on the stage
at my feet the whole set. A lot of the crowd had driven down from
Cleveland, and we played a great show, one of our best." Stiv Bators,
the Dead Boys' colorful front man, was originally from Girard and
graduated from Ursuline High School on Youngstown's north side.
Harold "Happy" Chichester, bassist in the Columbus-based funk
band Royal Crescent Mob, still remembers the Cedars audience:
"The Youngstown crowd could be serious drinkers, and shows at
Cedars might be a little more raucous and wild than in, say, Akron
or Toledo ... I could be wrong, but I seem to recall the crowd being
right there in front of us on the same level, which I think is kind of
cool.  It makes for real interaction, which, depending upon the energy and intoxication level, can be good or bad."

The next two decades brought successive waves of local, regional,
and national acts to a still empty downtown. In the early 1990s,
I would be among the college kids crowding up against the stage,
spilling $1.50 Rolling Rocks on sticky green linoleum, or shouting
conversations in the back by the jukebox. Our movements depended
on the music. Sometimes we bobbed up and down to Boogie Man
Smash. Other times we swayed like hippie-mamas to the mellow
vibe of Rainbow Tribe. One night, I marveled as I watched a young
man light a row of candles across the front of the stage. At Cedars,
artistic freedom sometimes trumped fire hazard.

In November 1993, I got to see Cracker at Cedars on the "Kerosene
Hat" tour, just as the hit song "Low" broke into mainstream radio.
That night, I was surprised to see the line of patrons snaking all the
way down Hazel to Federal Street, a sight I hadn't witnessed before or
since. It was cold outside, but the small bar was hot and packed. Front
man David Lowery performed almost the entire show with his shirt
off, his reddish-blond hair matted with sweat. Twenty years later, I
contacted Lowery at his University of Georgia email address, on the

off chance that he remembered this night in Youngstown. Lowery continues to record albums with Cracker and Camper Van Beethoven and teaches in the University of Georgia's Terry College of Business in a music business certificate program. He surprised me with his recollection of Cedars as a venue: "Cedars was your typical dive bar.... But it's this kind of minimal PA in a small room that gave birth to the rock 'n' roll ensemble ... I personally believe bands sound better in these rooms if they don't play too loud."

Cedars did not always have a house sound system, which—as I learned from my musician friends—is what transforms a bar into a music venue. To get a better sense of Cedars history, I spoke with Pete Drivere, house sound manager at Cedars since 2001 and owner of Ampreon, a locally based recording studio. Drivere said he started frequenting the bar when he was 15 (in what he dryly calls the "pre-MADD days"). He began performing with the Infidels, the legendary Youngstown rock band he founded, at Cedars in 1981, when they set up their own equipment in one corner of the bar. By the mid-1980s, Tommy Simon invested in a sound system that soon made Cedars a much sought-after venue for area bands. A vibrant local music scene began to grow around Cedars; groups such as The Infidels, Thee 8 Balls, and B-Minors soon attracted out-of-town followings.

"People started driving in for the uniqueness of the music," remembered Drivere. In the late '70s and '80s, there were no other bars in Youngstown that booked live, original music; clubs typically featured classic rock or heavy metal cover bands. By purchasing a sound system, Tommy Simon would establish Cedars as the only bona fide live music venue in the heart of downtown Youngstown for the next three decades.

For me, Cedars also has represented a haven from the materialistic suburbs. Once the site of a chapter of the United Steelworkers of America, 23 North Hazel Street became a destination for blue-collar bohemia, attracting a clientele of local artists, writers, and musicians. "If you want to have a conversation about French cinema or anything creative or artistic in Youngstown, Cedars is the place," said my friend Demos Papadimas, a musician and songwriter who performs at the bar. Transcending decades of trends over the years, Cedars became a beacon of hipness in a town too well-known for crime, corruption, and economic depression.

Over the years, a kind of lore surrounded the building itself. In the early days, bands played upstairs on the second floor until a fire damaged it. I once heard that the upstairs ladies' room was decorated with hairnets from a defunct beauty shop, and the men's room with old 45s. There used to be peeling bordello-red velvet wallpaper, which I heard some ripped away as souvenirs before it was removed. Even the stage had its own aura. My friend Jeff Sirkin, who played at Cedars with his band Cap'n Courage in the 1990s, told me he "was very excited to play on the same stage where once upon a time the Goo Goo Dolls (in their original Replacements-y punk incarnation) had played." I heard rumors that the Ramones hung out here after playing at the much larger venue, The Tomorrow Club, a block over on West Federal Street. (I picture lanky Joey looming over a beer at the bar, the red light casting a diabolical tint over him.) Poised by the cash register and liquor bottles, erotic clay sculptures of men's torsos, created by local artist Scott Pergande, encouraged rock and roll Bacchanalia.

Cedars's structural features also held important clues to the city's history. In 1995, the ceiling tiles were ripped out to reveal ornate tin ceilings dating back to the Gallagher Building's beginnings as a liquor store in the early 20th century. That year, Tommy Simon purchased the Renner Building property next to Cedars to build a patio area. After the Renner was demolished, a pile of rubble was left in the corner. That same night, after a show at Cedars, my brother Mike, future husband, Corey, and I each took a brick from this pile. My brother's love for this bar and for downtown Youngstown is such that he drove around with this brick in his Chevy Cavalier for years. Even after he moved to Chicago, he kept this memento of home.

---

Cedars has been a local institution for three generations, but its status hasn't made it invulnerable. Its charm as a dive bar ultimately sealed its fate in December 2012, when the Gallagher Building was sold to developer Dom Gatta III. He purchased the building to make way for renovations that would complement a trend of downtown revitalization. Cedars was ousted from the Gallagher Building because of what Gatta said were structural problems. In the *Vindicator*, Gatta said, "Cedar's will not stay there. ... With all the upgrades and everything else, it does not fit my vision for the building." Gatta said he planned to renovate the Gallagher to include apartments, offices, and an upscale restaurant.

Underground Youngstown's shock and anger reverberated on the Internet. That December, one Twitter user adopted the handle "FakeDomGatta," whose bio read: "Your one stop shop for gentrification. Officially unofficial. Ruining everything since 2012." A series of farewell shows were performed in January 2013. In the spirit of bon voyage, patrons were invited to pick up Sharpies and cover the walls with good-bye graffiti.

Not long after the announcement, Mara Simon, Tommy's daughter and current owner and manager of Cedars, promised that Cedars would have a new home. In March 2013, it reopened as Cedars West End on 706 Steel Street, not far from the brownfield where the long-defunct Ohio Works of US Steel was located. It occupies the space of a former Irish bar, the County Maigh-Eo. Mara and partner Billy Danielson carefully planned out the interior of the 1929 building in homage to 23 North Hazel Street. Drivere was consulted on the floor plan. The original wooden bar was reinstalled in the same wrap-around form, and Pergande's torsos still decorate the bar. In the men's room, someone even took the time to re-copy a line of graffiti that survived for years at the old location: "I seen Greg Masely fuck Greg Miller out of hate." In the women's room, a smiley face is drawn by the greeting, "Hey beautiful."

Although the downtown location has been so closely associated with her father, I am told that Cedars West End is "Mara's thing." Demos Papadimas also told me that the new location is still sought-after and well-booked in advance. The old guard of the 1980s is returning to mingle with new audiences. In 2013, the Infidels inaugurated the West End with a rare reunion show, and Thee 8 Balls recently performed in memory of bandmate Dave Tarazewski.

When I informally polled patrons about their feelings about the move from downtown, the consensus seemed to be that everyone has moved on. Drivere told me, "I notice about 95 percent of the regulars come to the new location. [The controversy] has definitely died down."

If everyone else seems to have moved on, am I the only one who feels a deep sense of loss?

At first, I was reluctant to visit Cedars West End. When my husband and I finally made it to Steel Street, I wasn't sure if we found the right place. There was no sign, only the painted Guinness advertisement I recognized from the internet. Later, when I asked Cedars promoter Aleisa Drivere if she knew why there wasn't a sign, she paused for a moment and answered, "It's part of the mystique." When I asked the same of Bill Lawson, executive director of the Mahoning Valley Historical Society, he pointed out, "If you remember, for many years, the old location didn't have a sign either." The implication seemed to be, if you need a sign to find Cedars, then you probably won't understand it anyway.

When I stepped into the new space, there was no smoke, but I immediately recognized the old wooden bar, the red stage lighting, the pinball machine, and the bathroom graffiti. Instantly, I knew Cedars could never be the same for me. The imported interior details felt more like a commemoration than an invocation of old magic. Like a child is to her parent, Cedars West End is, and should always be, definitely "its own thing."

At this time of this writing, the Gallagher building still awaits redevelopment, its cornices still stamped "1904." Amidst any urban renaissance, dive bars are an endangered species, their futures jeopardized by the same code violations that make them cool. As Lowery said to me, "Funky comes with the territory." If things went down differently, and Gatta decided to gut and rebuild Cedars in the

Gallagher Building, wouldn't it still lose much of its mystique?

It's true that the old Cedars, punk rock, and the downtown Youngstown of my youth are long gone. But they live in our collective memory. Maybe all that anarchy and memory is growing and mutating into innovative forms by new generations of songwriters, rebels, and urban planners. Maybe Cedars West End is transfiguring the legacy of a local institution in the same way.

# YOUNGSTOWN, SONICALLY REDUCED

*By Nick Baker*

**W**hen I was a kid, I wanted to be a professional baseball player, a witty intergalactic smuggler, a famous
cartoonist, or some combination of the three, essentially an Omar Vizquel-Han Solo-Matt Groening
hybrid. But I always counted on that just being my
day job. By night, I would be a rock star. Not necessarily a musician,
just a rock star. That was where my heart was. This plan existed in
various incarnations throughout my childhood, which took place in
Liberty, a suburb of Youngstown's north side. I never learned an instrument or how to read music as a kid. When my grandma brought
me a ukulele from a trip she took to Hawaii, I just assumed it was
a guitar for someone my size, and I strummed that thing so hard to
my dad's Michael Stanley Band cassettes that I busted all the strings.
I didn't care if I couldn't play it. I don't even think I thought about
actually playing it. It was about the look. I was Pete Townshend in a
pair of L.A. Lights.

By the time I was a teenager, however, my mentality had shifted
from "be a rock star" to "kill rock stars" under that fundamental
punk tenet. I guess I secretly still wanted to be a rock star, just one
who didn't publicly believe in the concept, which was a standard
paradox you might hear through the PA system at a punk rock show
while packed in with a bunch of sweaty teenagers on the less-cool
side of the security guards and barricades.

Stiv Bators of the seminal punk outfit Dead Boys grew up in
Girard, another Youngstown suburb that neighbors Liberty. Every
Thursday, his parents came into the Avalon Gardens, the north side
Italian restaurant where I worked during high school. A good friend
and fellow employee had a plain black hoodie with a stylized "DEAD
BOYS" hand-painted on the back in neon green. When he wore it to
work one day, they introduced themselves to both of us. They were

super cool and very kind, and we had a certain reverence toward them. Stiv, née Steven, joined the Dead Boys in Cleveland, and the band eventually left for New York City. People who remember him nationally or internationally say Stiv was from Youngstown, not from Girard. So Youngstown always seemed pretty punk to me.

In high school, I started my first punk band with my childhood best friend and a guy he knew from his school. We played real shows, often at pizza shops and skate parks but sometimes matinee shows in bars. We played Cleveland several times. We played the Splash on Youngstown's west side, which would become County Mayo, and then ultimately, Cedars West End. Both my dad and the bass player's dad had brown Chevy Astro Minivans, and we got rides to our shows in those.

The bass player wasn't totally into the punk thing, and wanted to go in a different musical direction, so the band ended not long after my 16th birthday. But punk rock was my thing. I covered my blue Squire Stratocaster in band stickers, and I wrote songs that mimicked the politicized, anti-war, anti-Patriot Act spirit of the early W. Bush years. I once wore a black Adidas wristband turned inside-out over the sleeve of my white polo uniform shirt as an anti-war protest at Ursuline High School. I was told to take it off. My mom had made the decision to send me to Ursuline High School, even though I didn't feel that a Catholic institution was the best place for my new, spirited opinions. At least Ursuline was in the city, and it gave me a reason to hang around there. I grew up in Liberty but came up in Youngstown, with its steamy urban stink, bleak alleys, and cool bars. Youngstown had the Royal Oaks, Cedars, and Nyabhinghi, bars where bands I liked played.

I made friends with kids who lived on the north side, and that was where I spent my time. We snuck into the North Side Pool at night. We knew people working at the Dairy Queen across the street and they would let us in the back door to hang and eat hot dogs and Blizzards. We would go to Crandall Park in the middle of the night, smoke weed through a pop can and lay in the grass on the backside of a hill when a car drove by slowly in case it was a cop, which it often was. And though I suppose a slow moving non-cop car is theoretically scarier, it wasn't to us. We would go to the open-late Walgreens, get snacks, and roam around some more. I'm not saying Youngstown wasn't dangerous, but we never really worried about it. During the summer between my sophomore and junior years, we were having daily afternoon front porch hang sessions at a buddy's house on the north side after leaving summer class. It was hot. We were bored. So we started a band.

I was still in high school, but this band felt like a more serious project than my first one. We thought we were edgy. We went downtown on a bitter-freezing day in February in probably 2005 and took photos in front of shuttered buildings with mean looks on our faces. We were about as successful as four 16- and 17-year-old pseudo-punk Myspace astronauts could be.

---

It was Homecoming 2009 at Kent State University. Then-university president Lester Lefton was giving a speech on the front lawn of the Delta Upsilon frat house. It was about 11 a.m. My thrashy new punk band was drinking 40-ounce beers and making a live record in our living room, homecoming be damned. We made so much noise that alumni and current frat brothers were gawking at us through our windows.

By this point in my life, I was starting to really be involved in Youngstown's music scene. I lived in Kent but came home often. My band was gigging regularly. We played the Royal Oaks, we played Cedars, we played DIY warehouse shows and house parties and we were staples of the "punk, etc." scene. I had also recently embarked on another new happening, and that was a sort of punkish approach to hip-hop. Like any good white '90s kid, I had a cursory knowledge of rap music. But when I got exposed to underground rap weirdos like Del the Funky Homosapien and MF DOOM, I started to feel like I wanted to try it. Rap music and punk music have a lot of parallels, and it appealed to me much more than playing solo with an acoustic guitar.

The underground rap stuff was in my wheelhouse, and I took to the art form quickly. I made the kind of introverted, emotional, singer-songwriter-type hip-hop that white hipsters are comfortable with, and performed with enough aggression and punk ethos for the rockers to dig it. What this ultimately meant for me was that I could do this act in the bars, too, right alongside the rock acts. I was welcomed, and I definitely recognized a sort of white privilege that came with my ability to be successful as a rapper in Youngstown. The city was changing.

Downtown was deemed an "entertainment district," a designation the civic authorities—and real estate development concerns—had been hoping for because it meant more liquor licenses. This led to a few new business ventures downtown—an offshoot of a popular local Italian restaurant, a martini bar, and a coffee shop and art gallery that moonlighted as a music venue.

After graduating from Kent in August 2010 and doing some traveling, I returned home in spring of 2011. I got a job at the aforementioned café/gallery/venue, a spot called the Lemon Grove. Specifically, I created my own job handling booking, promotions, and media relations for the venue, doing my best to grow it and help it thrive.

We cultivated something fresh, something that had so much kinetic energy that we overestimated how much potential was left for more. For a time, we were cruising. We were operating the coolest club in town, in an area that was basically an urban desert in previous decades. Alcohol flowed freely and back patio weed smoke drifted into the parking lot. It was a social club as much as it was a venue. I kicked it there when I wasn't working there. The bands liked dealing with me for the most part, and I was able to meet a ton of active musicians in the area. I played my own shows about once a month, and pulled in many of those same people, at first by means of shameless self-promotion. But it went far beyond me, and the scene felt electric and tangible. Robert Frost wrote something relevant about this. It was referenced in a popular novel about teenagers and class differences. It involved gold and impermanence. And it was pretty applicable to the situation at hand.

There was a run, one that essentially bookended the summers of 2011 and 2012. During this period, I was knee deep in the greater movement that increased Youngstown's musical visibility, both regionally and nationally. I was also actively touring with my own music and making connections that would bring people through town later. Indie artists would reach out to us, the word now spread through the blogs and the online fora. I spoke with touring artists who would say things like, "I talked to [speaker's peer] and he/she said we had to come to Youngstown," which they often did, passing on Cleveland and Akron or even Columbus. We threw a successful mini-festival, the First Annual Youngstown Underground Hip-Hop Festival. There wouldn't be a second.

It wasn't perfect, even when it was great. Crowds are fickle, and The crowd often wasn't there to see the music and would prefer not to pay to get in, but, for a time, was willing to pay the cover if the spot was happening, which is obviously a chicken-egg conundrum. Also, certain types of music, including more mainstream forms of hip-hop and less ear-pleasing punk, metal and experimental electronica, were marginalized by venue ownership and turned away disinterested bar patrons. Taking a risk and booking an artist that was an unknown quantity was happening less often. Self-serving often seemed more important that scene-building. Things got shaky.

We had a pretty good operation for a while. We pulled in interesting artists and interesting art, which in turn fueled a desire to bring in more artists and more art. We had a philosophy to keep building. Keep converting the potential energy into kinetic energy. Keep growing the scene. We didn't think about hitting the ceiling. But when we offered high guarantees to national acts, relatively famed and obscure alike, and then fell hundreds of dollars short at the door, we ate the losses. The weekend crowds were thinning, and the weekdays were awful for sales. There was a strange new weekend warrior crowd that was starting to come downtown each Friday and Saturday night. That crowd wasn't there to build up downtown so much as it was there to use it as some kind of twice-a-week adult playland. All of a sudden, there were fights—and cops—everywhere. The weekenders were also dispersed among too many bars, most of which had no live music and therefore no covers. People stopped wanting to pay our covers—an issue that is still part of Youngstown's ongoing indie music war—and we would have to do free shows and pay the artists out of bar sales.

And while we struggled at times where I worked, the real blow didn't happen to us. After 38 years of being the only rock venue that really mattered in Youngstown, Cedars left downtown in the midst of a complicated fog of real estate dealings, increasing rent prices, and the sale of the building. The artistic crowd was swift and vocal in condemning the sale and the actions of the real estate people, and though it was significantly more complicated than it was initially made to be, a line was drawn, with the art folks who thrived on the affordable nature of downtown on one side and a new investor-backed consortium looking to sling drinks and turn profits on the other. Cedars moved to the west side—and still operates as the premier (and only) indie venue in town—and you could hear the bell tolling. In a move that was definitely in the works prior to Cedars's move but suddenly felt incredibly reactionary, the venue where I worked relocated to a much bigger building down the block, an extension of the more, more, more philosophy from the fatter times. The cozy confines and practical setting of the old spot never translated to the new spot, which felt ostensibly like a hotel lobby. The regulars and semi-regulars didn't feel at home and then stopped coming as often. Shows were booked less and less. By the following year, at least three more indie venues were either shuttered or stopped booking shows. By the end of 2013, downtown gallery-and-vintage-store Greyland was the only venue left, and it only hosted occasional DIY shows and did not have a liquor license.

---

In the fall of 2014, I stood on a jetty in Brooklyn, taking a photo to send to my mom. The photo was of the former Idora Park carousel, or "Jane's Carousel," the ride that survived the fires of Idora and was later relocated to Brooklyn Bridge Park.

I was there because I had chosen Brooklyn over Youngstown, too. My childhood best friend from my first band took the trip with me to help move my stuff to an apartment that I never saw before moving in. I didn't have a job, but I had musical connections in NYC. Youngstown was a becoming a bit of a drag, and I didn't want to live so far from my girlfriend, who decided to move to New York for graduate school. So I bolted from Youngstown, like Stiv Bators did in the late '70s, like my parents did after I was born, like the carousel did after the fire. I played roughly 15 local shows a year in 2012 and 2013. In 2014, I maybe performed five times. The bands and artists I used to play with were mostly kaput. Some were just elsewhere.

Youngstown had gotten pretty disheartening. The high point was a show at Cedars West End on the Saturday after Thanksgiving. It was basically a big reunion, comprised of a reformed-for-the-event band and a few other musical members of the Youngstown diaspora. It's bittersweet when the best show you participated in for a given year was a show that likely won't ever be replicated because the performers had either left town or hung it up. That show fostered a nostalgic trip back to a time when anything was possible, when downtown Youngstown was our home base and geographic limitation was something at which to scoff.

You learn a few things about population density in a place like New York City. A good Tuesday night indie rap show featuring only local talent at a DIY venue with relatively lousy sound will bring out 50 heads and other rappers who aren't on the bill but want to support. By the time I'd left Youngstown, I felt like the only indie rapper there. Not only was there was no indie rap community, the larger independent musical community of which I considered myself a part barely existed either. I was a big fish in Youngstown. But any apprehensions I had about being in a bigger pond faded when I realized that pond was like-minded, engaged, and sustainable. I may or may not stay in Brooklyn forever, but I don't see myself going back home, either.

There is a sense that everyone coming up in Youngstown leaves eventually. Clearly, Stiv saw the potential in the move because you don't relocate your band to a bigger market if you don't believe you have some kind of future in music. "No future" is another standard punk rock tenet, albeit a dated, contrived, Sex Pistols-style one that doesn't resonate much with me anymore. I don't think it totally resonated with Stiv, either. Punk rock can be contradictory. There are, and always have been, bands and people putting in time, energy, and money into the art form while maintaining a nihilistic, "no future" attitude. It asks, "Why bother?" while simultaneously providing many people with the answer to that very question.

Punk doesn't always encourage growth within itself, and changes in style or sound aren't always welcome. People attach their own purposes to punk—some are purists who want things a specific way and are not open to change. Some are looking for unique artistic expression outside of the mainstream, and some simply hope to latch onto punk during its more prosperous times to ride the wave and make a little cash before moving onto something new that the kids like more.

After all these years, Youngstown still seems pretty punk to me.

# IN THE CENTURY OF SILENCES

production of words was cut
to save money. First adverbs
and adjectives became seasonal,
but never returned. Then transitive
verbs—nothing an object any more.

Eventually the city was down
to just nouns and connective threads—
a tapestry already half unraveled.

After layoffs, only prepositions
and articles remained like baby aspirins
held tenderly on infant lips.

Expressions of love balanced
awkwardly on the tongue:
the *a* above a *the*, with a *beside*
underneath the *toward*,
an *after* behind the *before*.

When the plant closed, no
exclamations were heard,
but the city opened with the pink
of a thousand gapemouths, all
of its citizens miming themselves.

*Rochelle Hurt,* from *The Rusted City*

A late-night fire consumes the abandoned
St. Mary's Byzantine Rite Church on
Youngstown's west side. *Nicholas Serra*

# STICKS AND BONES

*By Gordon Murray*

The crumbling asphalt of Trumbull Avenue stretched for a little over a suburban mile between US routes 193 and 422. No one who lived in between the two main roads called them by their numbers. To us, the crosshatches at the top and bottom of Trumbull were Belmont and State. Hang a left on State Street or a right on Belmont Avenue—it didn't matter. Both roads would take you to the same place. In 10 minutes, you would be in "Murdertown, USA." I didn't know about the car bombs or the Mafia when I was growing up here, so it was just "Youngstown" to me.

I lived on Summit Street, a short, dead-end chip-and-tar spur that hung on the north side of Trumbull. We were a five-house, one-mobile home neighborhood. If Trumbull Avenue was the tree trunk, Summit was the narrow, middle-aged branch with bark missing, all but snapped off near the end, before it could grow any longer.

Tod Woods Elementary School and Lamancusa's Bar marked Trumbull's halfway point and at the bottom was Youngstown Sheet & Tube. The mill was so long that it seemed only to have a middle. On the other side, the Mahoning River wound and stretched. It was long and hungry, home to hellbenders and mudpuppies. Everything you can think of was dumped into it—truckloads of trash, piles of scrap steel, chemicals and bodies. The river swallowed it all.

I didn't know anything about death when I took aim at Frankie. He was the second oldest boy in an Italian family of eight, but his oldest brother, Leslie, died before I was born. He had two older sisters, two younger sisters, and two younger brothers. In the few remaining photos from our childhood, Frankie was always the one standing in the middle, smiling. I can remember posing with him and his brother David in front of our television set in the living room of our old house. It was my birthday. I was sporting a new cowboy hat and leather holster. David wore a ridiculously small birthday sombrero on top of his round head while holding some kind of party favor. His bib overalls were still wet with ice cream or spilled Kool-Aid. Frankie was in his spot between us, one arm each around David's and my shoulders. A belt hung on his small waist for two toy pistols that could fire rolls of paper caps.

Over the years, I must have shot Frankie hundreds of times. I just pointed the gun in his direction and pulled the trigger. I didn't think much about it. Once in a while, I'd aim for his legs to allow him opportunity to expire in a more splendid fashion—like in the old Westerns and war movies we watched on TV. Secretly, we all knew being wounded was best, since it provided extra time for the rest of the neighborhood platoon to arrive and watch the performance.

Most times, a loud, convincing moan was enough to set us all running in the right direction. Depending on whose yard we happened to be in at the time, it may have required several convincing and successively louder moans to attract the attention of those of us who might be cooling off with a drink at one of the neighbor's garden hoses. Eventually, all interested parties appeared on the scene, with the ultimate reward reserved to the fallen comrade on the ground. Having waited, and poised himself for a particularly dramatic death—he would perhaps crawl towards a dropped rifle, loudly toss off a final curse at the arrived enemy's ears, and grandly expire with a twitching leg. If there was sufficient time to plan, the shooter and shot might re-enact the last few moments to coincide with the arrival of the rest.

Just like on television, all-important action occurred in slow motion. The special effects were just part of our mutual dream—necessary because when one guy got it, it usually ended the whole war. We also played a lot of kickball and baseball, usually a day after someone found the last ball hit into the woods. Many of the lost balls were discovered while playing army.

Like most kids, we would argue about anything in the moment and forget about it in the next. Was it a strike or a ball? Did his foot really step out of bounds? Frankie had a few years on us all, so he could usually hit a little farther and win most arguments.

I don't think any of us ever figured we would go to college. Frankie saved himself the worry and decided when he was old enough, he would join the navy, just like his dad. The next time I remember anything about him is when he returned to school wearing his bell-bottomed sailor blues. His only hall pass was his sailor cap perched at an angle on his head. I think he managed to swagger to every class in session for the entire school day. I saw him in the bathroom combing his hair. I saw him in the cafeteria for lunch. We didn't talk much. He clearly had crossed over to adulthood and neither of us knew how to find the stairs back to when we were kids. He had learned how to smoke cigarettes while he was gone and he made sure to do this on the sidewalk after the bell rang and the busses started to arrive. He had one of those shiny silver Zippo lighters and he flicked it open and closed like a pro. He leaned against the school's brick wall like he just walked out of the officer's club on base. He took several long, conspicuous drags before one of the teachers politely asked him to clear off.

The next time I saw him he was dead. Almost 20 years passed since our last game of army in our back yards on Summit Street. There was no time to argue and no way to change a mind. I kept thinking, had any of us been there in time, he might have lifted himself up to shake the grass out of his black, curly hair and say, "Man, that was a good one. I think I heard my Mom calling, I'm gonna go home." But, this time, it was my Mom calling. Her voice was small and came from the telephone. "Frankie was killed in a truck accident somewhere in upstate New York … the family asked if you might be a pall bearer … you really should come home, but if you can't, everyone will understand."

I shot Frankie a hundred times and he always got up. I knew Mom remembered when Dad died, and what I said during the calling hours at McClurkin Funeral Home: "I'm never going to another funeral." I was nine years old, and I knew this was not how I wanted to remember anybody—especially my Dad. For most of the rest of my life, I managed to be absent from funerals. High school, college, and marriage increased my universe of potential dead friends and relatives. Even though I managed to ditch most of the events when they occurred, I never found a way to explain sincerely and respectfully that I just didn't want to go.

I would sit on the car's hood, or in the warm grass of an embankment, or behind a windshield streaked with slush and ice, and loosen my tie and wait. I would wait and listen for the fluttering sound of the miniature purple flags attached with magnets to the fenders of a line of cars that traveled the road like a train on rails. Then I would go home.

This time was different. The backyard battlefield that sometimes substituted for a place to play kickball, softball, and freeze-tag in the summer was full of grown-ups—strangers with faces who resembled people I think I must know. The funeral was over, and just about everyone around me tried to delicately balance Styrofoam plates with small mounds of pasta shells and slices of ham and cheese and maybe some yellow cake on laps as they ate.

They all talked in the low voices I heard after the church service. In my arms, I could still feel Frankie's weight in the casket I had carried down the steps of St. Rose's Church. When we were kids, bocce balls ticked in the grass and horseshoes rang on metal pins where the lawn stopped and the woods began. Now in the backyard where we grew up, occasionally someone would talk to me directly, and I would recognize Frankie's aunt or cousin whom I saw last at a summer cookout when I was a lot shorter. But, there were no mill rats, no lunch buckets. The air lacked the scent of sulfur and iron. The sirens on Trumbull Hill, the echo of pipes dropped in the rolling mill, and the whistle that signaled the shift changes at the Sheet & Tube were all erased.

I shook people's hands and mumbled things I thought grown-ups were supposed to say after a funeral, but I kept looking across the backyards to my old house. I was sitting on the edge of the wooden-plank floor of a deck Frankie's dad had added long after I moved away to go to college. It stopped just short of the apple tree that was third base. The gnarled tree seemed to have grown wider instead of taller. The branches were thick. The ground was decorated with the same apples that used to whistle from sticks on trajectories to the moon.

Each was a tiny green satellite launched in flight, powered by the determination of skinny arms and earnest hearts.  Some apples didn't quite slip the sky, and they fell with a satisfying whack on the metal roof of the Altronics building that still stood behind my old backyard.

Once in a while, I saw Frankie's mom. She looked ill though she pretended to be well, as mothers do. She offered strained smiles to those greeting her, but her dark brown eyes didn't seem to blink as the other people talked. This woman could bellow a call to supper across three yards with the note not diminishing until it merged with the traffic on Trumbull Avenue, but the time to call her son in for the night had passed. He was dead. Her voice now was just air slipping by a lump in her throat.

I wondered how long I could endure this day, and I wanted to bolt across the grass and jump the hedges into my own Mom's yard. A now grown-up friend of Frankie's younger brother walked out of the breezeway, looking for something to do. I knew he didn't know Frankie because he was talking just a little louder than everyone else. I sat alone and watched him. He spent most of his time in the kitchen and at the cookie table in the breezeway. When he wasn't eating, he just looked bored. Frankie was dead. He didn't seem to get it. He could have pretended to understand, but he didn't waste the effort. It was obvious no one from the family knew him. He would probably be out of here even before I was, which made me resent him even more. I was thinking about how it annoyed me that he was walking around like a tourist in Gettysburg. Just then, he sat down on the edge of the deck floor right next to me and said, "Hey man, how ya doin'?"

The sparse shade of the apple tree seemed to shrink to about half. I thought about how I might poke my plastic fork into him and watch as he shot across the backyard like a rapidly deflating balloon. Out over the middle of the patchy grass, his air would run out and he would plop into the dust of the worn spot directly across from the apple tree. It was still there. First base. The playing field had always been more of an oval than a diamond. Home plate and second base had always been farthest apart. The intimacy of the field allowed the occupants of first and third to engage in casual conversation during a game. I didn't feel like talking, today. As I twirled the fork around a lump of cake, I responded, "I'm O.K.," to the stranger who I realized had been talking to me for a while and chewing on a fried chicken leg.

I thought my few words would inspire him to move on to another attraction. I feigned tolerance and I expected my considerable effort to be rewarded with his swift absence. My brief acknowledgment of his presence only encouraged him. What blossomed was a chatty visit that would surely last as long as I sat on the edge of the deck floor— maybe longer. I wanted it to be time to leave. It wasn't. I wanted to walk home. I couldn't. There were so many people left, and others still arriving. Muted greetings, arms on shoulders, handshakes—"yes, I was one of the pallbearers." "I know, he was so young ..."

What else was I was supposed to do? Leaving now seemed so final. Maybe this was what made it so difficult to come in the first place. This was the world of adults. Here, was a place where a "do-over" was useless. I despised the strange person sitting with me in Frankie's backyard, but my chest ached when I thought of standing up to find a way back to my own life. Stepping in and out of the past should take more time. I knew what it was like when the last of the people were gone. I had spent time alone with memories of my Dad and the overwhelming abyss that replaced him. It paralyzed me. My deckmate's food and drink methodically disappeared in a cadence marked by bursts of witless chatter.

I was becoming desperate. My eyes could only fix on the freedom of the woods beyond the edge of the yard. It was about then that I heard something. A sound so slight it might almost go unnoticed. A sound like an angel's wings pressing fast circles in air—almost a song, or a soft single echo from a boy's choir that hangs aloft in a quiet church. It lasted only a moment. It was an apple falling. A greenish-reddish blur with part of the stem still attached. It streaked past in my peripheral vision straight down from a branch high above our heads. It almost whistled as it built up speed, but as fast as it appeared, it stopped abruptly, with a knocking sound as it struck the center of my deckmate's head. I turned quickly, just as the apple bounced in a simple elegant arc, twirling slightly from the top of his skull as if skipping from a miniature trampoline. I was in awe. A kind of rapturous giddiness began to overtake my body. It traveled swiftly from somewhere around my ankles like a bubble released from the ocean floor. It was gaining speed on a race toward the surface, spinning freely out of control, expanding, fueled by some divine force and the laws of physics, through my legs, my stomach, on a rhumbline to my brain where it would burst through my head and be freed into the atmosphere. It never made it to my brain.

If it had, I suppose I might have taken the opportunity to think about it. I might have contemplated what had just happened with an air of repose and dignity required of a grown-up in a crowd of grown-ups speaking in hushed voices. But as it passed my heart and lungs, I accidentally let it out. It exited my body in a gulping laugh like the one you get when you tell a joke at the dinner table and it makes your sister spit milk from her nose. It was loud and startled me into standing up. In an instant, it was over: the glances of others directed, I believe, at a piggish visitor yelling, "OW!" out of the blue, before spilling food and drink all over himself.

The next thing I knew, I was walking away from third base, and the apple tree. Muffled conversation had resumed behind me. I looked back once, and I almost tripped in the hole that was home plate. I thought I had stepped over it half an hour ago. But there it was, and just the right distance for a kickball rolling through grass, or a plastic whiffle-ball losing momentum momentarily. I continued right on through the next yard and on towards my old house. I could see the red picnic table with the often-repaired crooked leg still standing under the tulip tree by the back porch. As I cut through the row of hedges, I felt a low branch's thorn catch on the pant leg of my suit. It made me pause for just a moment, just long enough to wonder about that apple. Maybe it hadn't come from the tree branch at all, but from the skinny end of a faraway stick swinging circles at the moon. Man, that was a good one, Frankie. I guess it's time to go home.

# THE PRO-YO MOVEMENT NEEDS TO GET REAL

*By Sarah Sepanek*

I n the spring of 2006, I was kneeling in the dirt on the north side of Youngstown, in a community garden that had just been raised from the vacant lot across from my house. In what had been a tomb for a hundred old tires, I wanted to grow vegetables and hope.

I'd lived on Lora Avenue for a few years already. My car had been peppered with bullets, courtesy of some kids walking down the street in broad daylight. Gunshots rang out nightly. In coming years, two of my neighbors would be murdered. The economy was dismal. I had my doubts some red tomatoes and rose-colored glasses could change much. Being a journalist didn't help my optimism.

I knew jack about weeding and composting. But I was a Youngstowner, and I was in it for the long haul. I was told enough that I was too negative. I wanted to balance the negativity with some positivity. Growing tomatoes was a start.

After ripping rough weeds from their hold, I needed more compost. I scooped some into my bucket and spied something plastic mixed in with the dirt. It was a used syringe. Digging deeper, I found another. Then I remembered all the tenants that came and went on the corner of Lora and Ohio, the spoons that used to line the curb, ambulance sirens at 4 a.m., a panicked neighbor telling the paramedics his girl-friend was dying, and all the other neighbors and friends, desperate, addicted, sick, or dead. Then I remembered that a community garden doesn't mean shit to many people in Youngstown. The transparency of this symbolism bowled me over—a feel-good community project literally covering up a real, underlying epidemic that was eating our town alive. The drug crisis can seem like an insurmountable problem, but ignoring it in favor of pet PR projects wouldn't help. Where was the call for volunteers to start a needle exchange? These peppers and squash can't be better than that for the city.

In time, the garden proved to be an asset to my neighborhood; it is definitely a little less rough than when I moved in 10 years ago. It used to be that kids moved in so they could live out some gutter-punk fantasy—sharing some decrepit warehouse space and reveling in the street cred. Now, the appeal was do-goodery and public improvement. When I moved away in fall 2014, new neighbors would rather roast kale than shoot dope.

I'm comfortable attributing the influx to a changed perception caused by things like the garden, the Northside Farmers Market, groups like Stand Up, Fight Blight, and the hard work of the Wick Park Neighborhood Association. But perception is only half the battle. Some improvements merely play a shell game, repackaging "problem areas," especially those close to campus. So one street is a little better. What about the next block? And the next?

In Youngstown, what is window dressing, and what is true progress? The garden wasn't the first or the last "pro-Yo" project. In the early 2000s, this movement exploded because of social media, clever marketing, and the hard work of citizens no longer content to be the butt of jokes. The pro-Yo spirit fostered groups like the Mahoning Valley Organizing Cooperative, businesses like the Lemon Grove Cafe, and countless endeavors by local artists and entrepreneurs. Phil Kidd's Defend Youngstown became a brand, a credo, and a storefront packed with the best of Youngstown wares. There was more to do than just joke about how terrible everything was. Things were going well in Youngstown nation.

There were some clunkers. The off-ramps near campus were refurbished to make the university more attractive to parents and their wads of cash, as if to say faculty turmoil, rising tuition, and on-campus crime, step aside—we need a giant red "Y" on the overpass! (A "Y" that matched the YSU logo in neither typeface nor color, by the way.) But when a student hands over the next 30 years of her life to a loan company and drives past that "Y" every day, it shouldn't cause an existential crisis—"Y am I in Youngstown, again?"

Media has a love/hate thing with the Yo. On one list, we're one of the

Best Places to Raise a Family—the next, we're the Worst Paying City. Giant banners boasting the latest accolade adorn downtown. But before you believe *Forbes*, figure in the dismal school ratings (receiving an "F" in standards met overall in 2014). Coupled with the contradiction of being named one of America's Most Miserable Cities, the banners seem more of a George Bush/Mission Accomplished faux pas.

Case in point: *Entrepreneur Magazine* names Youngstown one of the best places to start a small business. Yippee! We've heard this before. The spin: This is good for Youngstown! The truth: This is good for business owners because they can exploit desperate people who will work for non-union slave wages. Rock-bottom real estate and tax breaks don't hurt either.

I don't want to see lists in banner form. I want results. I want a job that pays enough to pay for the gas it takes to drive to work. I want the majority of housing to not be owned by slumlords or con-victed felons. I want the city to properly fund services for the poor, the sick, the addicted, the elderly, children—to, you know, service.

Youngstowners are decidedly unpretentious. There's no point in pretending anyone is better than anyone else. We're all in the same boat, and it's a crappy boat, so we better band together for the rough seas ahead. I've broke bread with names that adorn museums and halls, had drinks bought with wallets much fuller than mine, shot pool with the mayor. That realism and camaraderie are needed to determine what projects are the most beneficial. Not a bunch of decorative delusion.

I don't see the quaint Historical District sign at the end of my street. I see a house my friend spent hours painting and decorat-ing. After she was forced to move because of the dank economy, the house now sits abandoned, windows smashed, curtains beckon-ing like ghosts. I see the walk my neighbor was wheeled down on a stretcher after he was shot. I see the burned pile of a homeless woman's meager belongings, destroyed in a porch fire. There's a red tricycle parked in the doorless doorway of a crumbling home, so on-purpose looking and maudlin that you expect to see a film crew of poverty pornographers nearby staging the whole thing.

Nobody invests time and money and energy because they saw a sign or a banner. They do it for love, family, friends, devotion, honor, and tradition. They do it so they can have a future, so they can be safe. They do it for their families. Everyone still on board this crappy boat has hope, and they won't give up the ship.

In the end, what we need is a Youngstown that doesn't hide its problems and aims to improve quality of life for all, a Youngstown that looks to the future while remembering its roots. If the entire community is tended to like the garden—and not buried if it doesn't make good spin—we will all flourish.

I started photographing the Iron Roots Urban Farm when it was little more than a large community garden. Today, Iron Roots employs several local residents, is partially powered by solar, and is producing food for local restaurants and farmers' markets. **Sean Posey**

In the last standing building that was once the Avanti Motors factory, fallen doors lead to an open field. *Matt Campbell*

I first met Terrie Hughes at a neighborhood clean-up in the then-embattled neighborhood of Idora. A lifelong south sider, Hughes is an active churchgoer, model, and mentor to local youth. *Sean Posey*

# FAMILY

# LIMINAL STATE

*by C Lee Tressel*

**W**e are riding in a convertible through downtown in the middle of winter.

I am 9 and in the thick of my Victorian phase, which means I wear prim white earmuffs and a peacoat that isn't heavy enough for the weather. Just a few minutes into the parade, I realize the trade-off I've made to look like the polished young lady I strive to be. I envy my brother's Starter jacket and my sister's stocking cap. They sit atop the back-seat and wave at the cheering crowd.

The city is a snow globe. I smile into the swirling wind at all the people, although I can't see anyone's face. I know the cheering crowd is not braving the cold for me; they want a glimpse of him and them—the conquering heroes, the local boys who have done the impossible. I am along for the ride.

The parade ends in Federal Plaza. We file onto a makeshift stage. I am pushed to the front so I can see, but I don't want to see, don't want to be seen by the thousand beaming faces. I want to retreat from the phalanx of speakers blasting nothing but bass. The sound truck parked nearby bears the image of a scope with crosshairs. There's nowhere to go.

With every introduction and speech, cheers echo louder off the brick walls. This is a big deal—a national championship is a big deal—to our family, to this town. I search hard for the elation every-one else is feeling but can't seem to find it.

During one of the longer speeches, I notice a man weaving through the crowd near the stage. He wears a beat-up Steelers stock-ing cap and days of stubble. He's skinny like Shaggy from Scooby-Doo. His teeth are in bad shape.

"Please," he says to everyone and no one. "Please ... someone help me."

The people around him look irritated but say nothing. They give him space so his grubby sweatshirt doesn't rub against them.

"I'm hungry," he says. "My family's hungry. Please."

I do not have a word for the raw pleading in his tone. He seems unaware that this is a celebration, that we're in the middle of being happy. We act like he isn't there.

"Please ... help me."

He is nearly shouting now. The people around him jostle and scold. I stare from my place on stage. Soon enough, a cop comes and pulls him out of the crowd. Bodies close the gap where he was standing. We are all relieved.

I lived my growing-up years in a beautiful residential no-man's-land on the edge of Youngstown proper and Boardman, a suburb. Because of my father's job at Youngstown State, I spent more time in the city than most of my peers. One could argue that running around the concrete catacombs of Stambaugh Stadium was not at all the same as hanging out in an urban neighborhood, but I had access to Youngstown as a place and a community in ways that my firmly suburban friends did not.

I might've been proud of this access if I had been aware of how unique it was or what it meant. I had a vague sense that not everyone drove north on Glenwood Avenue through Mill Creek Park, past Mr. Paul's Bakery and the Youngstown Playhouse, around the U-Haul building and over the Mr. Peanut bridge to get to campus. I knew very well that not everyone went to a college football game every Saturday or else listened to one on the radio while raking leaves or scouring the bathrooms or doing homework. Thanks to my father, we had the chance to move freely between worlds. He was welcome in both places; so, then, were we.

In my suburban world, I heard stories about the dangers of visiting "the inner city." I listened to grown women in my neighborhood admonish each other to lock their car doors and never stop at a red light when they drove downtown. I listened with a mix of fascination and confusion when they counseled each other to wear baseball caps so they would look like men and thus be less vulnerable to carjackers and other city dangers.

I was aware of the buildings with spray-painted plywood across their windows, the Foster Theater we were never allowed to go to with the puzzling "XXX" on its marquee. I saw the mammoth empty-looking warehouses and the Salvation Army building that, to my young mind, was either a military base or a Christmas factory that pumped out red kettles, hand bells, and felt Santa costumes. I was aware that a cop patrolled the entrance to the athletic offices inside the stadium and that the gun at his hip was real.

Then again, I never believed I was in danger. Even the sour-smelling man we often saw at the McDonald's by the stadium held the door for me. The first time he did it, my mom told us to say thank you and stop staring. Occasionally she would slip him a Filet-O-Fish when we left the restaurant. This was the world my parents fashioned for us: a world where consideration for others—and civility in return—was a given.

I was shielded from the difficulties of living in the Youngstown of the '80s and '90s. The suburbs were good to us. We had more than enough; we felt safe.

Having the chance to move freely between suburb and city influenced my perception of both places. Neither world was simple, I noticed, nor were the people in it.

I knew even then that my two worlds could never truly be separate. They spoke to each other, bled into each other. Even when we were living in the rural outskirts of a more distant suburb, the other world—the version of the city we knew—was never far away.

It is the middle of winter again, though a different winter and just as cold. I'm having trouble sleeping. I'm thinking about basketball practice and my seventh-grade crush and the tube of Revlon lipstick I'm hiding under my bed.

I go to the computer in the living room where my brother is fast asleep on the couch. The modem makes its racket and he stirs. He squints into the blue light of the screen then flops over, burying his face in the pillows. I hope my friends are signed on, but no one is. I pull my nightgown—a YSU football camp t-shirt that fits more like a dress—over my scabby knees and float in and out of chat rooms.

The phone rings, knocking me offline. The sudden noise sets my heart pounding, and I scurry to answer the call. I stand on the chilly linoleum in the kitchen and hold the phone to my ear. It's KC, a coach on my dad's staff. It's not unlike KC to call at all hours, but this time something is wrong. He doesn't chat. He asks for my dad.

I feel my legs carry me to his room. He's already awake.

"It's KC," I say.

I perch on the arm of the couch and try to listen in. He doesn't say much. I run my fingers along the mulberry plaid upholstery not knowing what is coming but knowing it's bad.

My brother sits up and asks why I'm hovering like a creep. Before I can tell him that it's KC on the phone, before I can explain that the hair on my arms are electrified, my dad emerges from his room in sweatpants and beat-up sneakers.

"I have to go to the hospital," he says. "It's gonna be OK. I'll be back soon."

A fire has started in the tips of my ears and is moving into my face.

"What happened?" my brother asks.

My dad hesitates. He zips his coat and looks at us long and serious.

"Jermaine was shot," he says.

"What?" I say, as if I didn't understand every word. "Is he OK?"

My dad shakes his head and stares at something on the rug. We wait.

"I don't know," he says. "I hope so."

The way he says it, I know Jermaine is already dead.

Jermaine Hopkins, one of my dad's players.

Jermaine, a smart kid from Winter Park, FL.

Jermaine, who could cook like a master chef.

My dad's face is drawn in a way I have never seen. My brother and I watch him go, his car tracing the gravel lane then heading for the city. We watch him as if the part of him that loved Jermaine was never coming back.

Over and over I pull the story of Jermaine's death from the cedar closet of memory and try it on like an old coat. It has always been too big for me, too heavy, and yet after all these years, I can't part with it. The weight of it—that it happened, that it was part of my life in Youngstown—I still need to feel.

For those of us who have ever lived in broadcast range of Youngstown, a violent end is a familiar story. We are not shocked. The names of the dead on the evening news are always just names—unless you know one of the people. Unless you knew him when he was alive.

I didn't know Jermaine the way his teammates knew him or the way my father knew him or the way Jermaine's mother did and so would miss him every moment for the rest of her life. Sometimes I doubt whether the story of Jermaine's death is mine to keep or mine to tell at all.

But this place is where I grew up: on the liminal edge of two deeply complicated worlds. In the Youngstown of my youth, the lives of people in these two worlds didn't often intersect. I was allowed to be in both places but felt rooted in neither. This betweenness, this both-ness have shaped who I am.

Youngstown—the place, the people—knows liminality, too. We know what it's like to be in the space between the old way and the new way coming. We know what it's like to forge a life between selves.

# IN LOWELLVILLE

*by Dominic Caruso*

The Our Lady of Mt. Carmel Italian Festival is held every July in Lowellville, a Youngstown suburb ensnared in the post-industrial valley near the Ohio-Pennsylvania border. To find the *festa*, drive east along the Mahoning River, past the shadows of the steel mills under the slush-colored lid of the sky, which no longer glows with an orange cast from the blast furnaces. Interlaced tree branches canopy over the road. Slight bends are sharper than they appear.

Even though I know the way, it is hard to shake the feeling of being lost. Just a few miles down the road, when I emerge on the other side in Lowellville, I always discover the same small, unassuming working-class neighborhood. I find a place to abandon the car, and I cross the bridge on foot, over the river and train tracks to where the festival is vibrating in the summer night.

Like most local Italian festivals, the *festa* has the usual food vendors, carnival games, and ramshackle rides. Old men shout numbers in Italian as they play morra. Other men play bocce on a court of crushed stones beneath the pavilion, the sudden clack of a forcefully thrown ball snapping the game and those of us watching out of our languidness. The Our Lady of Mt. Carmel Band plays Italian songs under a string of lights on the bandstand. The place is packed. Children run wildly. Teenagers roam unpredictably. Men and women sell food and raffle tickets, t-shirts, candles, and crafts.

I walk around, avoiding eye contact with the barkers operating the carnival games. I always lose track of time, but it doesn't matter because I'm there to see what everyone else is there to see. The *festa* includes a spectacle that, as far as I know, cannot be experienced anywhere else in quite the same way. Transformation, the kind experienced in dreams, can sometimes find its way into everyday life. It happens here, at this *festa*, with something called the Baby Doll Dance.

Local history—a *Vindicator* article accessed on the Mt. Carmel Club website—suggests that the Baby Doll Dance's Italian origins can be traced to Southern Italy, possibly Naples, and prior to that as a ritual imported from Spain. In fact, it's possible that the Baby Doll Dance as it exists today came to America through the efforts of one man, Michael Lucente, who came from Italy in 1905. After forming a similar Italian band in Aliquippa, PA*, Lucente started the Lowellville Mt. Carmel Band in 1927, according to Jennifer Johnstone in a 2011 article written for the *Journal of Band Research*. Although the tradition of the Baby Doll Dance predates Lucente's arrival in Lowellville by more than 30 years, he assembled the musical accompaniment for the doll from the combination of Italian military fanfares and his own ingenuity. Johnstone says his music has enhanced and fortified the spectacle of the Baby Doll Dance since 1927. The Our Lady of Mt. Carmel Band that Lucente started and nurtured for four years as its conductor and arranger continues to this day with members, new and old, still playing many of the same songs remembered from his original, now lost, notations.

The band is part of the delight of the *festa*, a happy, asymmetrical mixture of men and women, some in their eighties, some in their teens and twenties. About 20 members make up the band in any given year; they wear modest uniforms, and the instrumentation is essentially a smaller version of a marching band: saxophones, trumpets, clarinets, and flutes. They smile at one another between songs.

As the evening deepens into night, the band processes from the bandstand playing Lucente's fanfares and disappears into a nearby side street. The crowds begin to converge on the square of blacktop in front of the bandstand. Members of the local fire department begin a half-hearted attempt to construct a perimeter rope around the blacktop with some blue trash barrels and a length of yellow nylon rope, pushing the crowd outward. After about a half-hour of convergence, contraction, jostling for a good spot, and expansion around the perimeter rope, the fire department gives the OK. Someone within earshot—perhaps more than one person—complains that in the past, you could go right up and touch the baby doll, but not any more. The band processes back through the streets, through the crowd, and in front of the bandstand, playing the special song of the baby doll. It's an Italian fanfare that favors the band's trumpets and sounds distantly like the Chicken Dance in its repetitive infectiousness. In quiet moments, the song will come to you for no reason, from the recesses of your memory. Everyone claps along. At the back of the procession is the baby doll.

The baby doll is about 15 feet tall. It is a humanoid female figure that looks as if it could be made of papier-mâché. It has a bust, and its conical shape suggests a dress. A primitive face gazes out from a white headscarf. The baby doll's dress is green, white, and red—the colors of the flag of Italy. Painted on the dress is a number—something like 119—the number of years the Baby Doll Dance has taken place. The body of the doll is built with a small black screen, through which the person inside can see, though how much is anybody's guess. The person inside the doll is undoubtedly someone who lost a bet. In place of arms, the doll has long wooden boards mounted horizontally on either side of it, which are in turn wired with numerous fireworks. Atop the baby doll's head is a wooden stake, also mounted with fireworks.

The baby doll moves to the center of the square. Perhaps to build suspense—or perhaps as an opportunity to receive the last rites—the person inside the doll is momentarily released and the doll is set down on the pavement. As the band ascends the bandstand, the doll is lifted and replaced upon the shoulders of the person who was freed, and the lights are turned off as the fire department ignites the fireworks on the left arm of the doll. Once lit, the band plays the special song again. The crowd claps along, and the baby doll begins to dance around, smoking profusely, and spraying showers of sparks from its left arm as the pinwheel fireworks mounted there shriek and whirl. The closest row of festivalgoers is about 20 feet from the doll. Eventually the fireworks burn from the left arm across to the right. The fear that one may be hit with an errant firework or doused in sparks is palpable, yet everyone is singing and clapping. When the fireworks on the arms of the doll burn out, a slow fuse ignites and begins to creep up the stake mounted on the doll's head. The doll ceases dancing, and the person inside crouches to allow the base of the figure to rest on the pavement. The fireworks on the head then ignite and launch several heavy-duty skyrockets into the night sky with blinding, nerve-rattling explosions.

And then it's over. The smoke clears, the lights on the bandstand come up, and the baby doll is spirited away to a side street. A few people touch the doll before it goes. It's supposed to be good luck. Johnstone's article suggests that the Baby Doll Dance represents the burning of a witch. Speaking for myself—an outsider even though I was born and raised nearby—I don't know what the baby doll means. It's a figure from the realm of dreams, both a horror and a marvel of life.

I did not see it in person until I was an adult. My mother, who spent part of her childhood in Lowellville, would tell us about it occasionally—part of a rotating series of stories about her youth. From her uneven descriptions, it was difficult to conjure up an image that made sense. Before I saw it in person, the only picture I could form in my head was a kind of kaleidoscopic Chinese dragon.

And yet the basic elements of the spectacle were not unfamiliar to me. As a boy in the 1980s, I marched with the other kids in my CCD class in the Feast of the Assumption procession every August. The St. Lucy's congregation marched behind us through the streets of Campbell, and the old ladies sang a Marian hymn in Italian with shaky voices. Ahead of us, the ushers carried the statue of the Virgin on a coffin-like pedestal. She wore a garland of ribbons upon which numerous dollar bills were pinned. I pinned one of them on myself—a delicate operation for a child—when the statue was still in the church. Above our heads, the Virgin wore a crown of gilded stars. The expression on her upturned face confused and frightened me. On the altar opposite the statue of the Virgin was the statue of St. Lucy. In her left hand was a shallow dish in which we were told she held her disembodied eyes. In St. Lucy's Church, in the Roman

Catholic Church, in an Italian family, in Campbell, in Youngstown, in the Mahoning Valley, in the time after the collapse of the mills, this is a little part of who I was, then.

In the church, a child like me would get overshadowed by the older people, the stocky Italian men in their Lawrence Welk-era polyester suits, and matronly women in stiff barrel-like dresses, the fabric thick like curtains. The people who surrounded me like trees came from Calabria and settled in Campbell, another working class, east side suburb of Youngstown. Campbell is populated by Italian, Greek, Slovak, and African-American families. Everybody there pronounces it "camel." And minutes from Campbell is Lowellville, where my thoughts often turn in the summer nights, and also in the winter, beneath the skies the color of dirty slush.

In this way, I've come to think of life growing up in and around Youngstown as the experience of living inside the innermost of a series of nesting dolls, with each outer doll marking the inner ones in ways that are difficult to trace.

---

*Interestingly, Aliquippa (where Michael Lucente started and led his first band) also has a *festa* with a Baby Doll Dance. I've been to it, and it has some striking differences. The Aliquippa dance is performed by two dolls, male and female, and the dolls are more polished and almost regal-looking compared to Lowellville's more roughly hewn figure. The fireworks of the Aliquippa dolls are tamer, and the dolls dance on a stage far removed from the crowd.

# SOMETHING TO SEE

*Laundromat—Niles, Ohio*

His father died young
and his grandfathers were strangers
        across the sea, so it's the smile
        of an old tailor

that he describes so carefully
I can see it:
        this smile pressed
        and sharply folded

by my grandfather
who has outlived everyone
        he wants to talk to
        to the point that I suffice

this afternoon in Niles
in his high-ceilinged laundromat
        so full of steam
        that I can barely see him

but it is something
just to barely see a grandfather
        close his eyes
        like the lion before the movies

as his huge head falls
and swings back up
        to some insane summit
        from which he booms

"his smile was something
to see, do you hear me?
  It was something
  to see."

*Allison Davis*

# CRUMBS

*By Keith Gottberg*

On the covered porch of the two-story house in Struthers, my grandpa and I sink into the green cushions on the white iron lawn furniture. An American flag, the one he hung every morning and took down every evening, flutters in the wind. The shadows from the mailbox and a single tree stretch across the lawn. We hold our plates and finish the last of our spice cake.

"Do you know how to get the last few crumbs off the plate?" he asks me. A child of the Depression wastes nothing.

"No, Grandpa."

"You pile all of the crumbs in the center of your plate. Then you smash them together with the back of your fork."

I follow his instructions and easily scoop up the reformed crumbs.

I gaze up at my grandpa, at his sharp, German features, his strong chin, and dark, fiery eyes behind bifocals. He appears tough. When we played, he would smile and threaten me with a "knuckle sandwich" as I bounced around the backyard. At 8 years old, I believe a real man must look like this.

Lung cancer took my grandpa from me too soon. Clifford Max Henry Gottberg had lived 70 full years. The steel mill took half of them. I only got 13. I have pieced together bits of Grandpa's history since his passing. He served as a marine with a reconnaissance photography unit in the South Pacific during World War II. Grandpa retired from the steel mill, but he once worked a second job pumping gas to support his young family. He won a classic Ford Mustang but sold it so he could finance his small tribe. When Grandma's mom passed away, leaving her siblings in the care of her alcoholic dad, Grandpa took in the two youngest and raised them as his own. He was a simple, blue-collar man, yet hundreds showed up for his wake and funeral.

For two or three summers in elementary school, my parents drove me the five hours north to my grandparents' house and left me there for a week or two. I would spend hours splashing around in the Struthers public pool. I developed a love for Faygo Redpop, an unobtainable delicacy further south. Grandma fattened me up on homemade cookies and jam and fresh corn on the cob—I had free rein in the kitchen.

Grandpa and I took daily walks around the neighborhood. We went to the grocery store on Fifth Street to pick up eggs and bacon for the next day's breakfast. Sometimes, we walked a couple streets over, past perfect lawns and ordered houses, to visit my cousins. Although he was in his sixties and I was still a kid, I never had to strain to keep up. Our strides matched.

Once, when Grandma and Grandpa visited us in West Virginia, I sat next to Grandpa on the brown couch in the living room. On the Zenith TV, the pregame show carried on about the NFL game, a Thursday showdown between the Kansas City Chiefs and the Minnesota Vikings. Eager to impress Grandpa with my newfound love for the sport, I proposed a wager.

"Grandpa, I'll bet you a dollar the Chiefs'll win." The Chiefs had traded for my hero, Joe Montana, in the twilight of his career.

"Deal."

We shook on it, but Mom ushered me to bed long before I saw the conclusion.

The next morning, Grandpa presented me with my winnings. It took me a moment to remember the previous night's wager. No one would have blamed him for letting it slide, this playful bet, but a real man pays his debts.

I have no definitive memory of the last time I saw Grandpa. My mother filed for divorce in the summer after my 10th birthday. Our biannual trip to Struthers came even less frequently. I heard about Grandpa's cancer diagnosis and speedy decline only through phone conversations with my dad in the winter before my 13th birthday. It never seemed real. I never saw Grandpa lose strength. I never heard him gasp for breath in his last moments. When I glanced in the casket at his funeral, he may have looked a little thinner, but he still had that iron jaw, that strength. I feel blessed that I avoided the ugliness of his passing. He will always remain a legendary figure in my mind. He never suffered defeat; he simply advanced to the next level.

I followed Grandpa into the military. I saw Afghanistan and Iraq. I work hard at every job I have, giving 110 percent even when the retail giant I work for doesn't deserve it. I long for a local steel mill so I can live in his shoes, just for a couple of months or a couple of years. He never told me about his experiences in the mills, but this mythological shaping of steel has a romantic quality. Like military service, it feels like another rite of passage, another proof of forged manhood. The thought of working with my hands and crafting something lasting feels so much purer than stocking shelves. I want to understand him better, this symbol of masculinity.

The old man left the boy. The Midwest steel empire rusted. Yet from the scraps, something new emerged. Like cake crumbs on a plate, I have pressed his essence down and formed something new within me. At 30, I still believe a real man looks like that.

# A FEW COLD NIGHTS IN '58

*By Ed O'Neill*

**M**y dad decided to sell Christmas trees to make some extra money for presents. He had a partner named Guy Petruzzi who worked with him at Truscon Steel. They pooled their money—whatever they invested they couldn't afford—but the idea wasn't to get rich. Just get a little ahead. There were five of us kids and counting mom we were seven. I don't think Guy and his wife, Gayle, had kids—he was probably just helping dad out. They bought about a hundred Scotch pines, the only kind my father would buy. When he was a kid they never had a real tree. The thing they used he nicknamed "The Tobie" because it looked like a cheap, thin cigar sold during the Depression. It was made of wood and was about as tall as a hat rack. Had 10 or 12 fold out little arms up and down the length of it. They stored it in the closet and when Christmastime came, would take it out, put a few strings of lights and a box of icicles on it. My dad hated it and swore if he ever had a family, he would always get a real tree. Which he did. Sometimes we'd go all over Youngstown before he'd find the perfect one.

My dad and Guy rented a lot owned by Ralph and Carmen Naples right across from their restaurant, The Golden Dawn, on Arrow Street. They set a fair price; I think it was something like five to eight bucks a tree, and they were in business. Now they only had the lot for a week, so they needed to sell about 20 a day to make a profit. Well, the first two days they didn't do so good. Sold seven. But they figured as it got closer to Christmas, things would pick up. And it was cold. No business at all during the day, because the men were working and most women were home. So they had to be there at night—5 p.m. to 10 p.m. And it was cold. They'd stand out there for hours in the lot—with a little string of lights around it and a little fire going, but it was bitter cold. By the time Christmas Eve came they had over half their stock left so my brother, Tim, and I were recruited to help. I was 12 and he was 10 and, for an hour or so, we were all there together. Only sold eight.

My dad and Guy said they were going to go over to The Dawn for a sandwich. Told us to hold down the fort and sell any tree on the lot for a dollar. My brother and I stood there for two more hours and never sold a single one. We were nearly frozen stiff, so I went over to see what was taking Big Ed and Guy so long, and when I saw them at the bar, I knew they were drunk and had given up the Christmas tree business. Meanwhile, Tim saw some guy dragging a tree off the lot and he yelled and chased him 'til the poor guy dropped it and ran off. We always felt bad about that. Fella just needed a tree and didn't have a buck for one. So we finally got dad and Guy out of The Dawn and went home for Christmas.

# SAUDADE

*By Nikki Trautman Baszynski*

**W**edding soup. Brier Hill pizza. Monkey salad. These foods are incomprehensible by name alone to non-natives, but they are staples of a Youngstown diet. That's why, with just a quick scan of the menu from the new Columbus restaurant, Olde Towne Tavern, I knew the owners were from Youngstown. Making room on the one-page menu for these treasures could only be the work of fellow Mahoning Valley folks. And sure enough, owners Kevin Burns and Brad Hobbs hail from Canfield. Thanks to these two fellow Youngstown-area transplants, I now have a little piece of home readily available to me.

Having left Niles at 18 for Chicago, and later for New York, and then Columbus, I had become accustomed to missing these dishes. Although I enjoy dining in cities known for their cuisine, I relish even more the nourishment of Youngstown cooking. It satisfies a craving for not just the taste, but the feeling, of home.

For me, the pepperoni roll is the most salient symbol of Niles and family. For quite some time, my only trips home were for holidays. And, for as long as I can remember, holidays meant pepperoni rolls from Alberini's on 422. It was important that they come from Alberini's. Nearly everyone in my family had worked there at some point in time: my mother and father met there, my grandfather served as the accountant, and my grandmother spent 40 years as the office manager.

It was my grandmother who made it her personal mission to ensure that Alberini's pepperoni rolls were a highlight of holiday gatherings. Whether it was Easter, Labor Day, Thanksgiving, or Christmas, we knew we would be whetting our appetites with a roll. Even better, whenever I departed, she made sure to tuck one into whatever giant bag I was carrying, which allowed me to share this fare with college roommates, new friends, and co-workers.

When my friends in other cities would question my love of the pepperoni roll, I would attempt to explain an even greater creation: the Mt. Carmel Festival cheese puff. The cheese puff is simple, yet genius. Sweet, fried dough encompasses melted American cheese. It's a two-handed delicacy. My willingness to drive hours to consume one (OK, 10) of these seemed strange to my non-Youngstown friends—until they had one for themselves. During festival season, my Facebook newsfeed fills with pictures of the classic summer indulgence along with the laments of those who missed out. It is a shared love, those cheese puffs.

That love seems to also extend to another Youngstown essential: the cookie table. Legend has it that because Youngstown was a primarily poor immigrant town, families often were not able to bear the cost of weddings on their own. So instead of a cake, the entire community would join together to bake cookies for the reception. And though this practice was born of scarcity, the result was abundance, diversity, and an amazing tradition that has become an integral part of Youngstown natives' weddings. Outsiders find it to be odd—and then awesome. It is the inherent Youngstown tradition: coming from little and working together to be more. The kolachi, buckeyes, ladyfingers, and pizzelles are a constant.

Initially, food nostalgia was the closest explanation I could find for the relationship between Youngstown natives and the foods they love. But this description didn't quite fit. Nostalgia generally evokes a sense of the past, of childhood, and of days gone by. But, there is plenty about the food culture of Youngstown that is still very much present. I don't long for cheese puffs because they remind me of my childhood; I long for them because they are so closely connected to my understanding of what it means to be home. For those of us who have left, our nostalgia is not for memories of the past but a longing to be there in the present. It is a desire to join once again and partake in the best sustenance there is—a perfect union of food, family, and friends.

I found a better term than nostalgia for this relationship: *sau-*

*dade.* This Portuguese word has been translated by some to mean a longing to be near again to something that is distant. This longing to return home and experience home by way of its nourishment exists for us because of the community that has cultivated it. You can't have *saudade* for the food of your hometown when there is nothing particularly special or unique about your home to begin with. We owe our lasting connection to the parents, grandparents, and great-grandparents who have slowly and lovingly created the feeling we get when we come back and order cavatelli from Antone's, eat wings at Sunrise, enjoy Tressel Tortellini while reminiscing about Carmine Cassese at MVR, watch Fernando Riccioni work the massive line at Wedgewood Pizza on a Friday night, or buy a bottle of Charlie Staples Bar-B-Que sauce. Whether it's a blueberry donut from Whitehouse Fruit Farm, an ice cream cone from the original Handel's, the architecture of the B&O Station, or the view of the Mahoning from Anthony's on the River, food memories—both past and current—remind us of where we come from.

Like the cookie table, the diverse and varied history of Youngstown's immigrant families has resulted in a beloved collection of foods that invoke both connection and belonging. It's why community and church festivals continue to attract citizens from downtown and the suburbs alike. Everyone is celebrated and their food is shared. People come together for that food. And perhaps, more importantly, they come back for that food.

I feel fortunate to be able to sit at Olde Towne Tavern in the company of people who understand why the city is so special. And it lets me fill a void until my next trip to the Mt. Carmel or Brier Hill festivals to grab a cheese puff or plate of cavatelli. After all, if Youngstown food really does produce *saudade*, it will always taste better when eaten within city limits.

# THE ONLY CHICK IN TOWN

*By Diane DiPiero*

Chick Rushen was my grandfather. His real first name was John, but I don't remember a single person ever calling him that. He was an even-tempered, good-humored, loyal man who enjoyed a Budweiser and a cigarette in his breezeway after a long afternoon maintaining his beloved corner lot in Campbell.

Chick was a smart kid, but he had to leave school as a teenager and take a job in the steel mills in Youngstown to help support his family. He didn't complain but got to work mastering the deafening cutting tools at Youngstown Sheet & Tube.

Years later, when a freak accident caused one of the machines to spin out of control, resulting in Chick losing his four fingers and thumb on his right hand, he took it in stride, learning to write, shake hands and swing a golf club like he had been born a southpaw.

For his entire life, he wasn't the guy who used to work at Sheet & Tube or the guy who lost half his hand working in the steel mill. He was Chick. Dependable. Funny. Generous. His life was simple but his personality, like his name, was distinctive.

In the early- and mid-1900s, what Campbell lacked in bucolic majesty or architectural refinement it made up for in ethnic flourish. Inside the nondescript, modest, brick or wood-frame houses that lined this small suburb of Youngstown, European cultures thrived. Potato pierogi were stuffed and boiled every Friday in one house; cavatelli and meatballs prepared every Sunday in another. As the years passed, foreign languages were still spoken by second- and third-generation family members, even while slang phrases and Americanized accents slowly crept in.

Although from a variety of backgrounds, the men of Campbell shared a salt-of-the-earth disposition and a get-it-done attitude. These traits no doubt made it tolerable to work in the sweltering blast furnaces of the steel mills. They also produced a culture of people who spoke plainly but passionately about everything from national politics to neighborhood disputes.

Nowhere was this plainspokenness more obvious than in the nicknames acquired by many of Campbell's men. Their monikers told it like it was, identifying each person for a distinct physical characteristic.

Legs was tall. Shorty was not. Puffy and Jumbo were plump, while Beak had a large nose. There was Head and Bumps, too. It was easy to figure out how most of these men had gotten their names. And even though I'd never learned the official story of how my grandfather acquired the nickname Chick, the few times I'd seen him in short pants led me to conclude it was because his legs were pale and scrawny like a chicken's.

The men got their names at a young age and carried them throughout their lives like sources of pride, not pieces of an injured past. There was no insult in being identified by height or girth or the shape of your extremities. These names were a part of them.

Millworkers blended into an unidentifiable sea of gray walking across bridges to the Sheet & Tube, their personal lives indistinguishable to the higher-ups who sat in comfortable offices. But later in the day or on the weekend, as they had a beer at Valley Cafe, ate at a St. Michael's steak fry or a St. Lucy's spaghetti dinner, or played 18 holes at Countryside Golf Course, they *were* their nicknames. Unlike the smooth, uniform bars of steel they helped to form at work, these men had chips and flaws, and those fashioned who they were.

It wasn't just steelworkers, of course. Schoolteachers, shop owners, salesmen: Anyone who was a part of the Campbell crowd could have a colorful sobriquet. In a community overflowing with Johns, Tonys, Mikes, Billys and Als, a guy had a chance to stand out as a Legs or a Jumbo.

On September 19, 1977, when the Youngstown Sheet & Tube shuttered its Campbell Works plant, a black-and-white filter immediately darkened the lens through which residents viewed Campbell. The orange glow that pulsated in the night sky over Campbell as steel was being made vanished, leaving a somber gray in its wake. Even the grass and the trees managed to lose much of their luster. The livelihood of a community had vanished, and its gritty, tough-as-steel people stood stunned.

But their character survived. Legs remained Legs; Beak would always be Beak. Perhaps the monikers were even more important now; the people of Campbell needed their unique identities as the livelihood they crafted slipped through their fingers. Somehow, they remained who they had always been.

Most of those men are gone now, including my grandfather. Like the 20 miles of factories that lined the Mahoning River, they exist only in memories. Most guys in Campbell go by their real names today. But ask anyone who can remember when the sky pulsed orange and you could watch beams of steel being made just below the Center Street Bridge, and he'll tell you there was no time like that in Campbell, and there was nothing quite like the unique band of men who made the town what it was.

Not too long ago, I ran into an old family friend while I was visiting Campbell, and we got to reminiscing about our families. His eyes got a faraway look and his lips turned into a familiar smile as he talked about my grandfather. "There was only one Chick," he said to me, his mind obviously filled with long-ago memories.

"You're absolutely right," I replied. "And there won't be another."

# A LEAGUE OF OUR OWN

*By Lori Tamburro*

As a child, I liked to explore the outbuildings on my grand-parents' property in New Middletown. One day, I was hoping to find the latest litter of kittens when my search took me into the brooder house, a small, rectangular building with white wood siding. By then, the brooder house was no longer filled with baby chicks—or kittens—but hanging on a hook just inside the door were old baseball shoes and a glove, both cracked from age and use.

Thinking they were my dad's, I ran to ask my grandpa if I could play with them. With a knowing smile, he sent me to ask my grandma.

I found her in the most likely spot for the late morning—the kitchen, where she was preparing lunch. When she saw what I had, she asked what I was doing with *her* baseball gear. At first, her tone was gruff, but with every question I asked, she became more light-hearted. Lunch was forgotten that day; Grandpa had to fix himself a sandwich. My then 60-year-old grandma and I went in search of the rest of her memorabilia.

In her youth, Grandma was a baseball player—one who made the newspapers. She and I spent the rest of that afternoon, as well as many afternoons to come, poring over her treasure trove of newspaper articles, souvenir programs, and team pictures.

My grandma, Anna Marie Sopko Molnar, was the daughter of John and Anna Sopko, Slovak immigrants who met in McKeesport, PA, and married in 1913 after a two-week courtship. Upon arriving in the United States, John moved to Youngstown but later relocated to McKeesport after learning two of his brothers were living there. After his brothers died in workplace accidents, John moved his wife and young family back to Youngstown where John had many friends. The family eventually moved to a house on Manhattan Avenue on the west side. John and Anna would have six children together. Daughter Anna was born in 1916. She was the second child and the oldest daughter.

The industrious family, like most then, did what they could to make ends meet. John worked at US Steel, Ohio Works, but he also butchered livestock for area farmers and raised canaries that were used as early carbon monoxide detectors in homes. The family often took in relatives who were new to America, so they could gain traction in their new nation. John would even give haircuts to friends and neighbors who later pitched in and bought him a barber's chair.

Anna, as the oldest daughter, had to look after her younger siblings and be the voice for her parents, who were still learning English. Outspoken, outgoing, and active, Anna naturally gravitated toward athletics, and her friends were other girls in the neighborhood who played sports, including baseball and basketball. Many of her neighborhood friends later became teammates and coworkers. Baseball would shape their childhoods, friendships, employment, and social activities.

According to a newspaper article and a souvenir program I found, organized girls' baseball was first started in Youngstown in 1923 by the Playground Association. The playground league began with four teams: Front Street Markets, South Side All-Stars, Mazda Lamp, and East Side All-Stars. Around 1936, the league grew to become the Youngstown Girls Baseball Association with sponsorship from *The Telegram*, a newspaper that was later absorbed by *The Vindicator*. Popular teams of the day were Bud the Tailors, East Side All-Stars, Fithian Insurance, Haselton All-Stars, Hollywood Dress Shop, Lispscher Senators, McKenzie Tire, Motorola Radio, Moyer Manufacturing, and Scher Tailor.

A scene in *A League of Their Own*, a 1992 movie about professional women's baseball starring Tom Hanks and Geena Davis, shows an African-American woman throwing a baseball to one of the professional players. The scene underscores the exclusion of blacks from the game at the time. Youngstown proved to be much more progressive in its amateur leagues, with at least two African-American teams, South-Side All-Stars and Haselton All-Stars. Although the teams were segregated, the games were not.

Anna, along with her friends, started playing on the playground teams on the west side and later joined the Youngstown Girls Baseball Association. She played on various teams throughout the years, such as McKenzie Tire and Fithian Insurance. In 1936, in the midst of the Great Depression, she was able to trade on her baseball skills to score a job as a seamstress at Moyer Manufacturing, a trouser manufacturer, and a spot on the company-sponsored softball team. Her baseball career with the Moyer team culminated in 1938 with local, district, and state championships and a trip to Chicago to play in the 1938 National Softball Tournament. Sadly, they lost to a Detroit team.

I never tired of hearing my grandma's stories and looking at all of her memorabilia. I loved the pictures the most. The ladies all looked so confident and determined in their uniforms, which resembled the men's uniform with short-sleeved shirts and loose, belted trousers or, in some cases, knee-length britches. You could feel the camaraderie and competitiveness and sense that they were having the time of their lives.

Through the pictures, I could imagine the things that I could not see but had only heard through family lore. I could picture my great-grandpa sitting stoic but proud in the stands, never missing one of his daughter's local games. I could see my grandpa, her boyfriend at the time, skipping out a little early from his shift at the mill to catch her game. I would wonder if grandpa's buddies who tagged along were hoping to meet one of her teammates after the game. I could envision the girls traveling to away games in Canton, Elyria, and Cleveland, as many as possible piled in a car and—as Grandma would claim—on the running boards, both hanging on for dear life and enjoying the rush.

It amazed me that women's baseball was so well received in Youngstown in the 1930s, even before World War II depleted the area's men's teams in the 1940s. The local games were often played at Evans Field and Rayen Stadium, and a typical softball game drew crowds of around 5,000 with championship playoffs having upward of 25,000 spectators. One newspaper article at the time commented on the popularity of the girls' baseball league in Youngstown and the thousands of fans coming to "witness a brand of baseball displayed by the so-called weaker sex that for interest and excitement far outdistances many masculine games." What was the draw? In the movie, *A League of Their Own*, a scene shows fans ridiculing women's professional baseball and the players. In Youngstown, whether fans attended to support their daughters, neighbors, and coworkers, or because the games were inexpensive forms of entertainment on warm summer nights during the Great Depression, one thing is evident from the sports coverage of the day—Youngstown fans loved their lady players. And those lady players loved the game.

The newspaper articles made these ladies sound like superstars in their day. Jenny Lindsay, Lil Parker, and Susie Sponseller were ace pitchers. Emily "Lefty" Blice was touted as the best female catcher in the area and a southpaw, too. Sisters Freddy and Helen Jakupcin, Agnes Samner, Carmel Carrozino, and Mary Hollis were known as heavy hitters. Anna Sopko was always good for a leadoff hit.

When *A League of Their Own* came out on television, I was so excited for my grandma to watch it, even though she gave up baseball long before the professional league began. After the movie was over, I asked her what she thought.

Her comment?

"You can't play baseball in a skirt."

# A GIRL'S YOUNGSTOWN

*By Jacqueline Marino*

I used to be afraid of the mills, or what was left of them in the late 1970s. Although I grew up in Boardman, my family often went to visit my grandparents on the east side. As soon as we got to the Market Street bridge, my sister and I would hit the floor of our mother's white Oldsmobile, clasping our hands over our noses and mouths. We would hold our breath until our lungs burned, until the structures we passed turned from smokestacks to skyscrapers.

My mother, a nurse, said the pollution the mills belched into the air made people sick and turned their lungs black. We didn't doubt her. All the old people we knew died of cancer. We weren't going to let that happen to us, though. When we saw the mills, we just wouldn't *breathe*.

Youngstown residents had been passing over the Market Street bridge—most of them much more happily—since 1899. After being fought by farmers who didn't want to develop the city and "big interests" who thought the bridge would hurt them, its opening was "the climax of one of the most romantic chapters in the history of Youngstown," according to a 1914 article in *The Sunday Vindicator*. The number of homes on the south side increased from a few hundred in 1899 to several thousand 15 years later. The number of schools more than doubled, and the number of churches increased from two to 10. Toward the 20th century's end, however, many journeys from the south side to downtown began reluctantly in the suburbs, whose residents, like us, were drawn not for business or fun but family obligation.

My sister and I continued holding our breath over that bridge throughout the 1980s, long after the mills closed. To us, the air was toxic and always would be. Those ugly structures were like sirens warning us to get to the air raid shelter. Mom would drive fast. We'd be blue, but safe.

As we got older, not breathing as we crossed into downtown

became a form of protest. Going to grandma's red brick house on South Pearl Street seemed like a form of punishment. In the house, we did little besides play poker for pennies and watch network television. Outside, my grandpa's garden took up most of the backyard, and we weren't allowed to climb the cherry tree.

Our grandparents' neighborhood was nothing like ours in Boardman. We rode our bikes everywhere, sometimes even crossing Route 224 on our own. We explored the woods with our neighborhood friends, playing hide-and-seek and climbing trees until someone was thirsty or bleeding. Our lives were full and free. Cancer, black lungs, stinky mills. None of that Youngstown would touch us. We wouldn't let it.

I didn't realize then that you don't get to choose what parts of your hometown you get to claim any more than you can choose your grandmother's green eyes or your grandfather's musical talent. You can't take the homemade cavatelli and leave the corrupt politicians, or notice the Butler but not the ruins. The Youngstown of my past is two cities: One safe, leafy, and full of promise, the other scary, dirty, and stifling. In my memories, in me, both remain.

I have lived in a half-dozen cities over the past 20 years. I have appreciated and criticized them all for different reasons, but only Youngstown feels complicated. Perhaps it is complicated in the way all hometowns are. They are the places where we learn to feel love and hate and the spectrum of other meaningful emotions. But I think it's different for those of us from Youngstown. Everything about our city is heavy—steel, corruption, racial and class division and, most distinctively, the weight of others' condemnation.

Everyone carries it, even those of us without direct ties to steel or organized crime. Neither Steeltown nor Crimetown had much claim on me. My parents were professionals, and my closest relatives to toil near the blast furnace were great-uncles. As a girl, I didn't see myself in the history of Youngstown everyone else seemed to know. Where was my Youngstown? It would be many years before I would realize no one had written it yet.

At my grandparents's house, there was no thrill of discovery in exploring the trappings of my mother's past. Almost nothing from my mother's girlhood remained—perhaps because she had so little as a girl. Her tiny bedroom, at the top of a flight of steep, narrow stairs, held only a single bed and a dresser. I knew kids whose bedroom closets were bigger. There was so little room, in fact, that the door only opened about halfway before hitting the dresser. I didn't know how my mother survived in that room. My bedroom was my refuge, the place where I read and dreamed and wrote in a household where no one except for my father ever wanted to be alone.

To write fiction, Virginia Woolf said a woman needed money and a room of her own. I think that's good advice for anyone wishing to write anything, though I would add another requirement: The room should be big enough for a desk.

Growing up, my mother did not have money or a desk, and she was rarely alone. Her one-bathroom, 1,000-square-foot house was shared with two younger brothers. My grandparents were very social and their neighbors were close. My mother remembers their community fondly. She walked everywhere, waving at the neighbors sitting on their front porches, engaged in the traditional Youngstown pastime of street watching. She even walked to her school, Sacred Heart, with its giant crucifix that towered over the mills. In the early 1980s, however, we weren't allowed to leave grandma's brick driveway. When we went to Sacred Heart for spaghetti dinners, we drove. Its school was closed by then and its crucifix had lost some of its majesty, overlooking the ruins of the mills we used to hide from in the Oldsmobile.

One by one, my grandparents' neighbors moved away from Pearl Street. There were break-ins and drugs. Empty liquor bottles and garbage littered the street. We rarely saw other children there, only our cousins when they were visiting from other cities.

My grandparents left for Boardman in the 1980s, and I didn't return to Pearl Street until nearly two decades later. I went back because Youngstown was haunting me. Once again, the city was at the center of something very bad on a national stage. By 2000, after a four-year investigation, the FBI had convicted dozens of people, including judges and other public officials, on corruption charges. Even its congressman, James Traficant, was being investigated. It was like the worker uprisings of the 1910s, the mob wars of the 1960s, or the economic devastation of the 1970s. It didn't matter if you had nothing to do with any of that personally. If you were from Youngstown, you felt the heat.

Corruption in Youngstown wasn't just a one-time thing. It was "institutional," woven into the fabric of its culture. Or that's what everyone was saying, anyway. As a graduate student, I wanted to learn why. I went back to Youngstown to research the places where the city's history and my family's history intersected. I spent many hours over several months interviewing my relatives, including my grandparents. Even though I found no close relatives among the scores of Youngstown politicians, organized criminals, and lackeys who have been convicted over the years, I was amazed by the few degrees of separation between my family members and those who have given the city its disrepute.

These connections were often brief but memorable. My great grandmother was shaken down for a gold pocket watch—the only thing of value belonging to her late husband—by a member of the Black Hand. Mobster Joseph "Fats" Aiellio, whose wife was one of my paternal grandmother's dearest friends, once gave my father a toy gun. (His mother, mortified, made him give it back.) My great-uncle Joe worked at the Calla Mar, a restaurant owned by Pittsburgh "godfather" Jimmy Prato, who threw a luncheon in honor of that grandmother when she died. At one time, almost everyone played the bug, the illegal gambling racket that perpetuated organized crime in Youngstown.

"Every day a guy would come to the house," my maternal grand-mother, Betty D'Onofrio, told me. "You'd play three cents or five cents on a number."

Even I have a connection to a Youngstown criminal. Briefly in 1992, I interned for Congressman Traficant on Capitol Hill. After a full day of opening mail, answering phones, and greeting visitors, I asked one of his female aides when it would be my turn to shadow the chief of staff and attend receptions and other events, like the only other intern—a man—had been doing all day. Her answer? Never.

"The Congressman always wants a woman at the front desk," she said, with a contempt I hadn't expected. If I wanted to do anything else over the next three months, she strongly advised me to find another unpaid internship.

That was my last day.

The next week, I walked into the office of the National Women's Political Caucus, a nonpartisan group that works to get women elected to public office, and asked the communications director to hire me.

She did, but only after a closed-door meeting where she told me to strike the Traficant internship from my resume.

"He's a laughingstock," she told me. "This will follow you."

Nearly a decade later, while doing graduate research, I found myself interviewing mostly women, simply because they tend to outlive the men in my family. I tried to get them to tell me more about the people they knew who factored into Youngstown's criminal past, but instead they wanted to tell me about what their lives were like in the '40s, '50s and '60s. They told me about baking pizzas in outside brick ovens and the dangers of hanging your clothes out to dry on the clothesline in Brier Hill. (If the ash got on them, you'd have to wash them all over again.) My grandmother's family was so poor they lived off fried potatoes and whatever they could grow in the garden. Still, they prided themselves on raising good kids. Once, when my great-uncle stole a chicken, my great-grandmother said nothing.

"She just looked at him in a way that made him feel so guilty that he took it back," Grandma told me.

These family stories were entertaining, but what about the mob? The corrupt politicians? The thugs that wired car bombs and shot people? I inched the recorder closer.

"They never bothered us," she told me. "They knew we didn't have nothing."

I understand why Youngstown's wives, sisters, and daughters

would want to forget the city's criminal past. It isn't really theirs; few women have emerged as perpetrators of the Crimetown USA image. In newspaper articles, they have been inconsequential characters, lightly sketched into the background, cooking or grieving. That's not to say they didn't know what was going on in backrooms and board-rooms, but you don't take too much ownership of the power struc-ture when you're just greeting people at the front desk.

Here were those two Youngstowns again. Instead of the free and the scary, however, I saw distinct male and female views emerge in our much-maligned city. The male one resided in the realms of collapsed industry and crime. It is the one known and vilified by the rest of the world. The female one centered on family. Though loosely referred to in references to the city's ethnic roots, its strong loyalties, and family values, that is not the story of Youngstown everyone else knows.

Despite the shame and defeatism many of us from Youngstown have felt, there is no badness in the blood here, no moral inferior-ity. There has been a historic lack of opportunity for half of us to speak for ourselves. Money and a room of their own? Few women in working-class Youngstown had either.

To write a creative work, according to Woolf, writers should strive for "incandescence," the state of mind in which "there is no obstacle in it, no foreign matter unconsumed." You can only get to it if you're free, even temporarily, of the emotions spawned of dependent rela-tionships, "grudges and spites and antipathies." We don't have to let our families in our rooms where we write, but we must let them into our writing. Otherwise, no one will know our past. Steel and crime do not reflect our experience. The things we want to talk about in our eighties, those are real.

As much as I disliked going to my grandparents' house on Pearl Street, it always smelled good. I often ended up in the kitchen, where there were always hard Italian cookies that never seemed to get stale and pots of sauce or wedding soup on the stove with my grandparents bustling around them, dropping handfuls of this or that into the pots, stopping only to let us kiss their pudgy cheeks and urge us to have something to eat. My grandparents' kitchen was as loving, happy, and gender-equal as any place I have ever been, definitely worth crossing the bridge for. I am sure it was just one of many oases in a turbulent city, but not recorded or celebrated as the special thing it was.

It's a small memory, but it feels good to write about it. Finally, I can breathe.

# CHILD'S PLAY IN THE CITY

*By Jack Bolkovac*

n the 1940s, there weren't many playgrounds or much organized recreation in Youngstown. Neighborhoods were the playgrounds for the children of the city. Ours was mainly Brittain Street and Poland Avenue, the Jones Street area.

Our immediate neighborhood had little grass. Our playground, for the most part, was our dead-end street. We were fortunate that there was no through traffic, and most families did not have a car. Our street was two blocks long. One block, where we lived, was concrete, and the other was a dirt road. Homes were only on the east side of the street. A.G. Sharp Lumber, Linde Air Corp., and Automatic Sprinkler Corp. were on the other side. Two-thirds of the families were first- and second-generation immigrant families, mostly from Eastern Europe. They were Croatian, Slovenian, and Slovak. On the dirt road part at the north end of the street, there were about six or eight homes that belonged to black families.

The men and older boys worked in the Republic and Youngstown Sheet & Tube mills. Quite a few families were headed by mothers whose husbands had died early from the rigors of hard labor. Given names were seldom used in our neighborhood. Almost every boy had a nickname, girls not so much.

In the 1940s, those families were made up of older teens and young adults, but there were several families that included younger children. The war took most of the older boys. Our oldest brother, John, an All-City football player, was drafted out of high school and died at 19 in a B-17 plane crash. Four brothers of our next-door neighbors served, as did most of the young men on the street. Some would return to marry. After the war, it seemed there was a wedding to go to every Saturday.

We grew up with little in the way of "the necessities" of sports. There were no playfields, few balls, few bats, and little other sports paraphernalia. Imagination and inventiveness provided most of the needed items for play.

In the spring, summer, and fall, we played most of our games in the street. Stickball, kickball, touch-football, kick-the-can and other games were favorites. Baseball bats were in short supply. They were usually souvenirs from organized baseball games. They would be given to kids who chased foul balls or were ball boys. If we had a bat, it was usually taped and had no knurled butt, which had probably broken off after someone dropped the bat too hard on the street. Baseballs, likewise, were often torn and held together with electrical tape. Stores sold what we called a "nickel rocker," a black, taped ball that sold for five cents.

Footballs did not last long on the street; when we did have them, the ends were worn, and the air bladder protruded. When the football finally broke, we would stuff the skin with paper. If we had no ball, we would make what was called a "sockie"—an old sock stuffed with paper or rags and tied at the end. Goal lines were usually telephone poles and the boundaries were the curbs. Touch-football was a favorite game on our street; you could play with four or five boys. If only two boys showed up, you could play a kicking or punting game. The goal lines were two telephone poles, and the idea was to punt the ball back and forth until one player was so far beyond his pole that he could not kick past it. It was important to catch the ball to prevent any roll and to kick straight.

Baseball sometimes was played on the street. For a serious game, it was only about a half-mile or so to Kryzan Field, a city ball field. There, we might find some other neighborhood kids and play a game. As long as we had five boys, we could play scrubs, two boys at bat and the rest in the field. When you made an out, the pitcher went to bat, and the fielders would rotate.

Our "toys" were usually not store-bought. We made most of them from wood or materials found in the neighborhood. One of the most common toys was a "rubber gun" made from a wooden board and an old inner tube from some father's car tire in those days before tubeless tires. We made a "gun" by cutting or carving the piece of wood to look like a pistol and using strips of rubber from the tube to hold the spring trigger. We used other rubber strips for the projectiles.

Not too far from our neighborhood was a large tree-filled area of about 40 or 50 acres, which we called "the woods." Our path to our schools (Bennett and Wilson High) was through these woods, all up hill, of course. In the woods were several hillside springs, the watering holes where we played. In the woods, we built ponds by damming up the spring water. These were our swimming holes in the summer and our ice-skating rinks in the winter. We built our own shacks.

Hoboes were a common sight in those days. These were men who had lost everything they had in the Depression. The hoboes had a large "shanty home" built of tin and scrap wood in a little hollow near a spring, which we stayed away from most of the time. Periodically, we did play pranks on them.

Between the woods and Gibson Street was a large city dump, which was usually a smoldering site where city residents dumped their trash. We sometimes made forays there to look for things we might use: bicycle parts, wheels, old crates to build shacks, and any other things we could put to use.

The *Our Gang* movies that became popular at that time pretty much described our neighborhood. We learned to share, and we did not have any fear of germs. Candy bars or bottles of pop would be passed around for all. But sometimes the guy with the goody would shout "No halfers!" and the rest of the gang would be denied.

Living in Youngstown at that time, post-Depression and during World War II, we had a sense of camaraderie, patriotism, and respect. We learned that in the neighborhood, our playground.

# INEXPLICABLE PRIDE

*By Monica Lott*

"Get out of Northeast Ohio," I told myself in northern Trumbull County in the late 1990s. I had my escape from Ohio all planned: undergraduate and medical school in nearby Rootstown would enable me to follow my parents' dictum that I go to college within two hours of home, but I had my residency planned for New York City and an apartment with my best friend all decorated in my head. I knew how many blocks we would be from Broadway.

My plans changed when I decided not to pursue medicine. As a student studying English and biology at The University of Akron, I still wanted to get out of Ohio. I told myself I could always come back. If I did stay, I wanted it to be because I was choosing to, not staying because I had no other choice.

A semester in London and travel around Europe saw me counting down the days until my flight home. Ties of family, church, and friends kept me in the area.

I went to school for my master's degree and doctorate because I had been told that education was everything. There were no more mill jobs. I ended up joining the new mill: education.

My relatives were never told that working in the mills was dangerous. These were the mills that made my great-aunts proud Rosie the Riveters. They were also the mills that my grandmother blamed for my grandfather's cancer. These were the mills that dictated their lives. My parents were married on a Sunday because that was the day her uncles were off work. And now I have found myself in other mills: first at a for-profit diploma factory teaching students who didn't know their degrees were more likely to bring them debt than a rescue from poverty. Now I teach at an accredited college. My young students are seeking better opportunities than their parents. My nontraditional ones are often trying to start over. Like my family members before me, I help put out a product.

I enjoy seeing those "Stuck in Ohio" bumper stickers, though I don't think I will put one on my vehicle any time soon. They remind me that others have made the same choice, whether they knew of their options or not. I have an inexplicable pride in this area, pride for our renown even when it's not for positive reasons. When my husband and I saw *Kill the Irishman* and the main character, a Cleveland mobster, responded with awe and respect to his girlfriend's Youngstown origins, I felt pride. Even though my mother heard that a mob car bomb had gone off not far from her apartment while she was working at the former South Side Hospital, I still felt a sense of connection to that character in the film. She was from my area.

I felt that same sense of pride and connection while watching comedians make fun of our congressman, Jim Traficant. He had come to my elementary school and sponsored one of the trophies I had earned for my 4-H project at the Trumbull County Fair. When I wrote my thank-you note to him, I promised that I would vote for him. He wrote back and thanked me for that promise.

In 2002, I voted for him, even though I really wanted Tim Ryan to win. My one vote did not make a difference, but the importance of keeping my promise had been instilled in me. Even if his hair, suits, and speeches made him the butt of jokes, he was known, and he stood up for his beliefs. His dishonesty resulted in his being expelled from Congress and serving time in prison, but the continuing assurance that he had been a voice for his constituents made him a popular character after his release from prison. In running for Congress again, he epitomized the Mahoning Valley's opportunity for second chances.

I understand why people leave, but I have come to feel that I would be breaking faith with my family and my history to give up the chance to share the legacy of pride, faith, and hard work with my daughter. These positive attributes may not be unique to Northeast Ohio, but I believe no other place could be more accepting of those who have failed and started over or as open to giving a second chance.

# MY ADOPTED GRANDFATHER

*By Stan K. Sujka*

I n my closet hangs a black, three-piece tuxedo that once belonged to a great man. In the inner breast pocket, written in magic marker on a Richman Brothers tag, is "3/30/40, size 46, salesman #5." It is the only thing I have that he once owned and the only thread that connects me to him now. I owe almost everything I have to this man. He not only served as a role model for me, he became a man I called grandpa.

He wasn't really my grandfather, but for me, a little boy of seven, alone in a new country with a new language, and new culture, Joseph Habuda became my adopted grandfather, or *dziadek* in Polish. Only now, many years later, do I realize how special he was, how important a role model he was to me.

At age 17, Joe emigrated from Golce, a town in the part of Poland once known as Galicia. His journey in the quest of the American dream led him to Buffalo, NY. There, at a wedding of a friend, he met Mary. Even though he was pursued, and even propositioned by another woman to get married, he told her, "I'm sorry, but I intend to marry Miss Mary Kornacki."

Once he made his commitment to Mary, he held her by his side for more than 60 years. Instead of going to nearby Niagara Falls, the honeymoon destination of the world at that time, he took his new bride to Youngstown for their honeymoon.

Joe and Mary decided to call Youngstown their home. They opened a grocery store on South Avenue near St. Stanislaus Catholic Church. They bought a small starter house on Wabash Avenue one block away from the store. While running the business, they started their family. First came Ted and Arnold, then Helen, Frank, Alice, and Joe Jr. As his family grew, so did my *Dziadek*'s business. He established a coal supply company, an asphalt business, and a builders supply company. I still remember how proud I used to be to see the big red cement trucks with white letters on their doors proclaiming "Habuda Supply Co." as they rolled down the streets of Youngstown.

*Dziadek* Habuda was a little more than six feet tall. The half smile he usually wore seemed to perfectly complement his round face. The first time I met him was when he came to Poland. At that time, he already was in his late seventies. His full head of chalk-white hair gave him the appearance of Santa Claus without the beard. He came to visit my *babcia*, my maternal grandmother, who was his niece. In typical Santa Claus fashion, on Sunday morning after church, he gave everyone he met walking back to my babcia's house one American dollar bill. In the early 1960s, one dollar was a lot of money.

Joe Habuda's generosity did not stop with the dollar. He became my family's sponsor to the United States. He spent time and money to help people like us. He gave without expecting anything in return. And we were only one of a handful of people Joe Habuda helped.

For more than two months, Joe and Mary Habuda opened their home to us. *Dziadek* drove us to his house from the Pittsburgh airport in his new powder blue 1963 Lincoln Continental. When we arrived, *Dziadek* made some spaghetti for me. It was the first time I had an Italian meal. I ate until my stomach hurt.

The next morning, he showed me how to make fresh-squeezed orange juice. I could not believe he threw the away the orange peels. In Poland, we only got an orange or two at Christmas, so my mama would grind down the peel, add sugar to it and use it as a spice for cakes during the course of the year.

*Dziadek* took time from his business and his family to help me. He never was too busy to sit down with me and answer my questions or take me out for ice cream. Until we moved out of *Dziadek*'s house, my adopted grandfather would drive me to school and explain the ways of my new adopted home.

On one trip to school, I saw a crossing guard blowing balloons out of his mouth. "How does he get all those balloons in his mouth?" I asked *Dziadek* with a curiosity of a 7-year-old.

He smiled. Slowly, with great patience, he explained to me what chewing gum was and how it worked. *Dziadek* bought me a piece of Bazooka bubble gum with a comic inside. It took a long time and much practice however before I learned to blow those balloons out of my mouth.

Joe Habuda's passions were life and family. Every year, even though we were distant cousins, my family was invited to the Habuda family reunion. As the Habuda family grew, so did *Dziadek's* pride and love of life. As a child, I was so proud to be included in his family and looked forward every year to that summer day of celebration at the Habuda family reunion.

*Dziadek's* love of life came from his love of God. He faithfully gave to this church. Every Sunday, you could find him in his best suit and tie in the second row on the left of St. Stanislaus Kostka Catholic Church on Williamson Avenue. At the age of 96, with his family by his side, he went alone to meet God. One last time he came to his church to say good-bye. Amidst the Polish choir and flutter of angel's wings, you could hear the prayers of thanks offered by all the people he had helped.

So Joseph Habuda's tuxedo hangs in my closet. He gave it to my dad as a present, but I have been the lucky one to wear it the most. It took me quite a long time to fill that size 46. Every time I wear it, it reminds me of him and of what it takes to be a great man. It takes love of family, commitment to one's wife, family, and business; generosity without expecting anything in return, friends, involvement in your community, a love of life, and a devotion to God.

Joseph Habuda had these qualities and the patience to sit with a lonely little boy of 7 and explain to him how bubble gum works.

At Calvary Cemetery in Youngstown, in the maze of roads and markers that fill the landscape like a city skyline, there is a memorial to my *dziadek*. As she had been in life for over 60 years, by his side rests his loving wife, Mary. I have stood in front of his tombstone on a number of occasions (every time I go back to Youngstown) and muttered words of thanks to him.

Next time, I go there, I may even wear his tuxedo.

*A version of this essay was first published in The Orlando Sentinel.*

# YOUNGSTOWN BORN AND BREAD

Sunday mornings, the smell of baking
leaks into the car as we drive to church
in the snow, rain, sun glaring, air
conditioner cranked, heat filling the van,
or wind whipping from an open window.

Mornings before work I smell stale smoke,
but afternoons it's there to welcome me
after good days, bad, fruitful lessons,
silence from students, irritation at my
own quiets sliding concentration.

I've made this journey daily with family,
friends, by myself, with a kiss and peace
sign to our departed in Lake Park Cemetery,
after arguments, or laughing, or tears,
sending me off and guiding me back.
Home is where it smells like bread.

*Sarah Burnett*

Serving the Youngstown

Carmine Cassese ...
Mahoning Valley Restaurant ...
the MVR building still occupies ...

Whether we were coming from a high-noon ballgame or one under the lights, my family and I would head down to the MVR after every 'Guins home football game, regardless of a win or a loss. "The restaurant," always warm and welcoming, has been a second home for my family, and we are among many others who share that same sentiment.

**Whitney Tressel**

In 2011, my friend and I made moss-graffiti "paint" in my blender and did guerrilla-style beautification on a blighted building near the Golden Dawn that didn't warrant any official attention. We blasted Lupe Fiasco's LASERS album and spent an afternoon painting a wall. That summer was a bit too hot though, so the moss died before it had a chance to grow. Even so, it felt really good to go ahead and do what we felt needed to be done, because, honestly, we can't wait around for strangers to take care of our neighborhoods. *Cherise Benton*

The work floor of the now-demolished Wean United steel plant near the Market Street bridge. *Matt Campbell*

WORK

# STEEL GRIT

*By Tom Kerrigan*

The year was 1976. I was a college student going down to US Steel to apply for a summer job. I had never been there before, but it was one of those places that lined the Mahoning River, over which I had driven a million times. Mr. Manche, a close family friend, worked in the employment office and had some pull when it came to hiring. I was only 19. My friends were getting minimum-wage jobs cutting grass and painting houses. So moneywise, this was a coup.

I had no responsibilities in those days. My biggest decision would be choosing the number of dependents I would claim on the hiring form. It would be zero or one, and all I knew was that it had something to do with income tax refunds.

"Drive an old car down there," Mr. Manche told me. The massive parking lot to the Ohio Works of US Steel, on Youngstown's near-west side, was a perfect landing spot for the airborne contamination generated by the mill. The automotive paint was no match for the corrosive nature of the emissions, which is why most people had a "beater" car they used to drive there.

I had given myself extra time to find everything because the street signs were covered with an orange crust that made them unreadable. The hue perfectly matched the color of the hot molten steel that bubbled inside the open-hearth furnaces, I would learn. The guard at the entrance registered me and pointed me in the direction of the employment office. When I arrived there, Mr. Manche, a man of diminutive stature, was running around the office. "I was six inches taller when I started here," he quipped. I filled out the application and put zero deductions. After my medical examination, I was directed to the onsite company store, where I bought steel-toed boots. An older man, wearing bulky pants with a matching green jacket, came in. He noticed me looking at his strange-looking outfit.

"It's made out of asbestos," he said. "There are some places around here that get hotter than hell. These keep you from catching on fire. You'll see."

A week later I retraced my route for my first day on the job. When I arrived, there were a half-dozen people gathered in the employment office: five guys and a woman whose name I cannot recall. I'll call her Martha. She was swimming in the smallest work jacket she could find, and her helmet was way too big for her head. The mill-issued safety glasses barely stayed on her face. Two of us were college kids; the others, including Martha, hoped to make a career of it. The mill had been around for almost a century and no one believed it would ever close.

A short, stocky man, with a black handlebar moustache greeted the new hires. "My name is Leo," he said. "I'm your foreman. I run the mason gang. Follow me."

The property went on for hundreds of acres, and Leo pointed out key buildings on our trek, including the blast furnace and open hearth. With a few exceptions, they were made out of sheet metal and broken windowpanes. Two cats ran by, chasing each other.

"Why are there cats down here?" I asked.

"They kill the rats," Leo said.

Although my family had a long history at the mill, this was my first glimpse into their world. I was awestruck.

Leo stopped between two squat, cinder block structures.

"There's the commissary," Leo said. "Not much there, just some vending machines. If you get asked to double-out, we'll give you tokens so you can eat supper. That other one's the clinic. We get bonuses for safe work days, so try not to go there."

We all nodded. To Martha, he said, "We don't have a ladies locker room out in the mill, so you're going to have to share the one in there with the nurses."

Being singled out appeared to make Martha uncomfortable.

"Any of you ever work in a steel mill before?" he asked.

"No," was the collective response.

"Some of these guys will try to get you to do their work for them. Don't let 'em."

Nodding our heads, we headed toward the furnaces. "There's one guy here, name of Wilson. I'd fire the son of a bitch if the union would let me. His crew's with us today, so remember, unless I told you to do something, don't do it. Some of these idiots make a game of it."

We went down to a sublevel of the large, open-hearth building. Even though it was daytime, the darkness required bright lights powered by gas engines. The air was cool despite the summer temperature up top. The work was already in progress. Outside the furnace were at least a dozen pallets of bricks.

He explained that the furnaces were made out of special fire brick and had to be torn down and rebuilt on a regular basis. Because the masons needed to get into some tight spaces, each one had two helpers. One was outside of the space loading the bricks onto the roller belt, and the other was inside taking them off.

We'd attracted the attention of the veterans who looked over the new employees. A tall man wearing all denim finished snipping off the metal bands that held the bricks onto the palettes. He came forward, pointing the large pair of cutters at the foreman. "Hey Leo, where'd you get these guys?" he asked.

"I don't know, Wilson," the foreman said. "You'd have to go ask Personnel."

"I'm asking you," Wilson said.

"Go to hell," Leo said.

Wilson approached me. "You. Who's your father?"

The question put me into a bind. My father had died when I was young, but my last name was well known. Since the Depression, my grandfather, followed by my uncle Joe, were general foremen of the open-hearth. Currently, my uncle ruled the place with an iron fist. I saw him off to the side, watching the work, his red hair poking out from under his gold helmet. He knew the culture better than anyone, so he kept his distance to protect me.

"My father?" I said.

"You heard me." Wilson said. "Who's your daddy? How'd you get this job?"

"My dad is dead," I replied. I was not going to give this guy ammunition to use against me.

Wilson shrugged and walked away.

"Over here," Leo said. "See these rollers? They're our conveyor belts. One of you takes the bricks off the pallet, two at a time. You put them on here and they roll down to the end. Your partner will be at the other end taking them off and building a little stack next to your bricklayer. That's all there is to it. Questions? No? Good," Leo said. "The thing is, you never want your guy to be out of brick. They get real cranky when they run out."

I understood the comment when I saw the bricklayers down on their padded knees in the crowded spaces. Leo assigned us to our posts. Well into the first pallet, I knew the hard and steady work was going make my arms ache that night.

The crew's world revolved around break time and, God forbid, you break the unwritten rule and work through one. At 10 a.m., most of the crew walked off for a smoke or a shit or both. Not surprisingly, Wilson was the first to take a break and the last to return.

Martha was positioned inside the furnace. Her mason had finished and was on his way to the restroom. Wilson watched her working.

"God damn bitch, taking a man's job," he said to no one in particular.

When Martha's partner took his break, Wilson walked over and replaced him. She was unloading the last dozen or so bricks from the transport. Wilson picked up a pair of bricks and sent them down the rollers to her, a clear deviation of workplace routine. She didn't notice that someone else was sending her brick, and kept stacking past 10 a.m.

Wilson picked up the pace. Instead of setting the bricks on the rollers and letting gravity do its work, he started pushing them, accelerating their arrival. In pairs, the bricks hurtled into the furnace. The increased speed caught her off guard, and one of her oversized gloves got pinched between two bricks. She turned to look back at the start, noticing Wilson for the first time.

A single mother of two, Martha was physically soft and without muscle tone. Her safety glasses were crooked on her face, perspiration causing them to slide off her nose.

She glared at Wilson through her thick, fogged glasses as she sped up to match his pace. The rest of the crew began noticing what was happening. Their chatter silenced as the challenge played out. The pallet was two-thirds empty as Wilson increased his speed. Barely able to keep up, she assembled the stack around her.

Smelling blood in the water, Wilson re-committed his efforts. The clanging of the bricks on metallic rollers grew louder and more constant.

Martha was bent at the waist, working in the confined space. Twisting from right to left, she was running out of room to stack any more. She looked over at the work area next to her, saw the men had left for break, and quickly switched sides of the conveyor. Within the larger space, she was able to spread her feet and work freely. She started building up the pile for the absent mason. This only served to motivate the muscular Wilson. His efforts were intentional and mean as he stepped it up.

Like a machine, she began to outpace Wilson, never allowing the bricks to back up on the rollers. On occasion she would slap her hands together with her oversized gloves, like a baseball catcher, eager for a pitch. Leo watched, along with 60 sets of eyes, all of us willing her to continue.

The breathing and sweating of the two warriors escalated. Martha unsnapped her jacket, exposing red suspenders that held up her pants. The pallet was near empty and everyone knew this meant survival to her. No matter what she had faced in her life so far, she had made it to this moment, and no one was going to take it away from her, certainly not this jackass.

With 10 bricks left on the palette, it was clear Martha had won. Eight, six, four … Wilson shoved the last two bricks toward her as hard as he could. When she unloaded them, Leo spoke up.

"OK, break time," he said.

Wilson lit a cigarette and strutted away, acting like he had only been doing his job.

Martha walked out of the furnace and removed her gloves and hard hat. The red bandana wrapped around her head was soaked. She wiped her face and neck with it, never making eye contact with anyone.

Wilson did not ask anyone to do his work for him that day but he did the next.

On our first payday, Leo handed out the checks. We newbies had no idea what to expect. I was shocked when I opened mine and thought of buying my friends a few rounds of beers. Martha looked at hers, turned and spoke her first words to me, "Now I can feed my family."

At the end of the summer, I went back to college with newly chiseled bricklayer's arms, pockets stuffed with cash, and Martha's payday declaration etched in my mind, like a mason's trowel gashed into drying concrete.

Martha and Wilson stayed behind.

# THE SCARFER

*22" x 30" linoleum block print*
*metallic black and pewter ink on paper*

I was just a kid, practically a baby, when my dad worked as a scarfer at Youngstown Sheet & Tube. I remember one day when he described his work to my brother and me. He said that when the steel came out from the molds, it carried imperfections from the process along with it—scraps of molten steel that clung to its sides. It was his job to "shoot sparks at the steel to clean it off."

In "The Scarfer," I imagined my young father as an angel, a celestial knight hovering above us all, riding along his sparks as we slept soundly on top of the valley. The lines that fueled his instrument became his wings in the glow of the molten steel. He transcended the dust and fire that made our reality, taking away the imperfections in an imperfect world. –Rob Hudak

# THE NICEST, MEANEST MAN: INSIDE JACK LOEW'S SOUTH SIDE SANCTUARY

*By Anthony Dominic*

"The person who has nothing for which he is willing to fight, nothing which is more important than his own personal safety, is a miserable creature and has no chance of being free unless made and kept so by the exertions of better men than himself."

*John Stuart Mill*

**E**ight o'clock Saturday morning, and the sun swells over the treetops behind South Market Street. Brilliant blond rays blast through rickety backyard fences and airy brick-walled alleys. Four or five sedans skate north or south, rarely turning, never stopping. Only the sharp October breeze lingers. It smacks of winter.

The strip of South Market running from the Southern Boulevard fork to the Mahoning River is lined with empty lots, hockshops, a porn store, and half a dozen shuttered businesses whose weathered signs have become relics of an era bygone. It's the kind of stuff that keeps most people moving. Residents will tell you as much; the strip sees little activity, especially this early. Except for the lone red-and-black painted building between Willis and Chalmers avenues—the South Side Boxing Club.

Jack Loew is around back, keying the padlocks to the gym entrance. He's a stout man of 54 with hairy arms and a fading mustache. His upper body is as strong as it looks, evident by the way he tosses open the garage door that leads inside.

"You learn to keep your shit locked up around here," he says, his grin uneasy.

The gym is dusky and cavernous. Its walls are covered in 25 years' worth of fight posters. No matter where you turn, the unwavering eyes of boxers come and gone are always watching, like deceased amateur Johnny Swanson, imprisoned lightweight "Dangerous" Dannie Williams, and retired middleweight Kelly "The Ghost" Pavlik.

Jack is known for his 20-year relationship with Pavlik, a hot-headed kid from the south side, much like the coach himself. Pavlik worked his way from Jack's first gym on Southern Boulevard (a closet compared to this one) to Caesars Atlantic City, where, in 2007, he upset Jermain Taylor for the World Boxing Council, World Boxing Organization, and The Ring middleweight titles . After a string of successful defenses, Pavlik lost the straps in 2010 to Sergio Martinez, broke up with Loew in 2011, and retired from the sport in 2013.

While Pavlik remains Jack's greatest prodigy—the embodiment of the Youngstown revival story, as national sports writers fancied him, for a time—the South Side Boxing Club preceded the former middleweight champion, and it lives on without him. In the next hour, it will fill with mostly young men from the neighborhood. Weights will start clanking. Heavy bags will start swinging.

"I see everything that goes on in this gym," he says, smiling, surveying the room. "We're real aggressive-type fighters, aggressive-type trainers. I'm always on their ass, but we have a lot of fun. I had this kid who once told me, 'You know, coach, you are the nicest, meanest man I ever met.' I thought, man, do I take that as a compliment, or what?"

Since opening the gym in 1989, Jack estimates hundreds of, if not more than a thousand, kids have passed through his doors. Some want a safe place to hang. Others want to get in shape. Few become amateur boxers, and even fewer become pros. But the doors remain open to all, regardless of age, regardless of skill, regardless of background.

What Jack doesn't advertise is that the gym, in theory, is a not-for-profit business. There are no steady fees, no filing cabinets packed with names and dues. There never have been. The only charge is $61 for a USA Boxing Passbook, a requirement for amateurs, which Jack purchases for those who can't afford them. The gym has lighting, heating, and running water because, from 6:30 a.m. to 3 p.m. five days a week, the married father of three works construction. After his shifts, he rushes home to let out his dogs before opening the gym from 4:30 to 7 or 8 p.m. On warm Saturdays, he runs an asphalting business. On cold Saturdays, like today, he's here, filling water bottles, readying hand tape, waiting for those doors to swing open.

---

Jack's first fight was on Glenwood Avenue, not far from his childhood home on the south side. He couldn't have been more than eight or nine years old at the time. The minutiae—why it started, with whom it started—have faded with the decades. But smart money says Jack won. He usually did. He never had the edge in height or reach, but the sandy-haired boy could move. He had balance and rhythm and a hard right hand from regularly pulverizing a stuffed duffle bag in his basement. After his fourth or fifth fight, word got around: Jack Loew could kick your ass.

This kind of reputation amounted to armor in those days. In the 1960s and '70s, the city's south side was teeming with gutty kids who, when not in school or at the dinner table, were running the streets. In the thick of pickup games, football or baseball, usually, personalities clashed. But none was as oversized as Jack's. He was as competitive as he was angry and aggressive. The kind of kid who was willing to throw clenched fists when one of his teammates was shoved a little too hard, or when trash talk turned to insults. More often than not, Jack remembers, he was bloodied defending friends, not himself, even when they flat out told him not to.

Jack can't explain his temperament, not even some 40 years later. His parents were strict but, for the most part, easygoing folks. His father, John, was a professional type, a longtime industrial engineer for the General Fireproofing Company on the north side. Jean was a stay-at-home mom, like most neighborhood moms back then.

Jack's grandpa ran concessions at the Stambaugh Auditorium, where crowds would flock every weekend to watch closed-circuit boxing from half a world away. Jack and his buddies, like future

International Boxing Federation lightweight champ Harry Arroyo, would bike uptown, and Grandpa would sneak them in through one of the auditorium's back doors. It was the closest a kid from the south side of Youngstown could get to the likes of Muhammad Ali, George Foreman, Oscar Bonavena, and Chuck Wepner.

"Guys my age didn't get to find out who won, who lost, until after the fact when their dads would come home," Jack says. "And even then, they never actually saw the fights. I'd watch them and think, 'I know I could do this.'"

When he was a teenager, Jack started training with local boxing coach Ed Sullivan at the old Naval Reserve Center near Cardinal Mooney High School. He remembers Sullivan as a vocal, "foot-up-your-ass" kind of coach, always honest with you about your strengths and weaknesses, always willing to put in just as hard of a workout as you were. Sullivan's old-school methods proved effective, too, as he produced Arroyo and future World Boxing Association lightweight champ Ray Mancini.

Jack's years as an amateur boxer (his record stands 18-1) were overshadowed by his success on the football field at Cardinal Mooney, where he graduated in 1978 as the school's then-third all-time leading rusher. Despite wanting to turn pro in boxing, Jack's father pushed him toward a football scholarship at the University of Southern Colorado (now Colorado State University–Pueblo).

In his first summer with the ThunderWolves, Jack took an awkward hit in practice. His knee fully hyperextended. After a rough operation and a slow recovery, the same knee was injured again the following spring. In an instant, both his scholarship and football career expired.

Jack moved home, bitter and aimless. One night, he went out to the Sugar Bowl, a bar on Glenwood. After a few beers, things went foggy. He started trading words with a guy he knew from Austintown Fitch High School. Then they were arguing. Then they were wrestling to the ground, yelling, pushing, kicking, punching. Next Jack knew, he was being handcuffed. It was over.

The night before Jack's court hearing, the nephew of the municipal judge hearing Jack's case was hospitalized after being battered with a baseball bat in a McDonald's parking lot. When Jack arrived at the courtroom, he had no idea what he was walking into.

Jack was calm, thinking the judge was going to dismiss his assault charges.

"But he goes, 'I'm tired of this teenage violence,'" Jack recalls. "'Sixty days in jail, probation, and a $150 fine'—and he got up and walked off the bench.

"It really woke me up, then," he continues. "The days of getting into a brawl and calling mom to get you out of the Boardman jail wasn't happening anymore. I might have been a tough guy on the street, but that was the worst, scariest experience in my life when they slammed those doors."

After 33 days, Jack was released from Mahoning County Jail. He would never start a fight again.

---

Night after night, Jack would drive home from his job with Tamco Distributors and pass a small building for sale at the corner of Boston Avenue and Southern Boulevard. Night after night, he'd imagine a little gym tucked inside with a small ring and a few bags. By the late 1980s, Youngstown's boxing scene was due for a pick-me-up. City gyms were closing; even Ed Sullivan had been displaced after the Naval Reserve Center shut down. And a decade of Mafia influence on the sport had spoiled many of the city's most-talented boxers, Jack explains. It's what deterred him from turning pro after he returned from Colorado.

"We had so many good fighters in this area that never got a chance because of these so-called wiseguys who ruined their careers, got them to sign into these ridiculous contracts that lined the pockets of these local mobsters," he says.

"There were a lot better fighters here than Ray Mancini, but Ray had the option of scooting out of town," he continues. "These other guys were stuck here. Jeff Lampkin, Greg Richardson, they did it, but they did it the hard way, and their careers didn't last long, and they didn't make no money."

When Jack finally converted the Southern Boulevard space into a modest boxing gym in October 1989, people thought he was crazy. Many still do. It's a labor of love in the truest sense of the phrase. He has always worked nine-to-fives to support the gym, and his boxers have often come before his wife and kids—a sacrifice his family, who understand his passion better than anyone, has often encouraged him to make. Many of his boxers he's clothed, fed, housed, and found jobs. His aim with South Side Boxing Club—though he never comes out and says so—is to provide everything the city once lacked in a gym. It's more than a gym: it's a sanctuary in one of Youngstown's long-troubled neighborhoods. It offers structure for kids who have none. It's a place where that south side aggression can be harnessed and given direction. Jack knows too well what happens when it's unbridled.

"30, 35 years ago, I could fight with you on a Friday night, and Saturday night we're gonna have a beer together—or we're maybe gonna fight again," he says. "But I never had to worry about you coming back and shooting me. You coming back and stabbing me. You getting 35 of your friends and beating me into a coma."

He hesitates, tugging at his chin.

"The south side didn't used to be like that. Now all these kids are killing each other now because, 'You said something about my mama,' or, 'You smacked me in my lip at school.' Man, well go punch the kid back; don't shoot him and kill him."

Sobering statistics back Jack's assessment. While the Steel City is no longer the murder capital, the south side was the stage for nearly half of the city's homicides in 2013 and 2014, according to Raids Online, the police department's crime-mapping service. Sifting through police reports and *Vindicator* articles, year by year, is dizzying—nearly every south side homicide is a shooting, and nearly every victim is a man under forty. It's a scene that seems to replay over and over and over.

"Our fate is already determined, somehow, somewhere," Jack says. "I could probably say our program saved some kids' lives. Or instead of 11, 12, 13, they didn't end up dead or in prison until 20, 21, 22. At least I got them through those years. But when they leave the doors, there's nothing I can do."

Jack says he returns to the gym day after day because he's chasing the next champion. His son, John, an assistant trainer at the gym, says it's more than that.

"He's bailed fighters out of our jail, given fighters money, 20 dollars here, 20 dollars there. I don't know if I could do it. Some would think he wouldn't—they just see an aggressive guy who swears—but what they don't see is a guy who teaches not just boxing but life lessons. He has the biggest heart in the world."

Jack is the reason welterweight Lavelle Hadley moved to Youngstown from his home in Springfield, IL, in 2011. Hadley had visited South Side Boxing Club years before, and after his longtime trainer passed away, he believed Jack would be the one to advance his career.

"Jack doesn't sugarcoat anything," Hadley says. "When I got here, I wasn't a really big puncher, and he straight-up said I was weak and needed to get stronger. 'These punches aren't going to hurt anybody,' he said, and he helped me with that."

In November 2014, Hadley won his pro debut by first-round knockout.

"There's something about the way he trains fighters," Hadley says of Jack. "He trains them to fight, to fight hard, and I like that. He catches mitts well; he has all the equipment you need. It's the best gym I ever been to." Hadley is in the gym five to six nights a week, every week, for at least three hours. After all that time, you get to know somebody, he says.

"Here and there, through all the aggressiveness, Jack does a lot for people," he says. "He has helped me out in a lot of different ways, kept me out of trouble. He is a very kind man."

John is convinced if his dad were in a sexy gym on the east or west

Coast, he'd be perceived as a Freddie Roach or Robert Garcia. A celebrity coach, always in the news, attracting aspiring boxers in droves.

"He never wanted to leave, and I think that says a lot," John says. "Other guys get handed [money] and will abandon you. Loyalty and commitment is big to him. And he instills that in his fighters. Where else do you see that?"

Jack Loew's South Side Boxing Club on Market Street.
***Sean Posey***

# HIDING THE EVIDENCE: IT'S A YOUNGSTOWN THING

*By Dawn Weber*

I borrowed his umbrella, broke it, then stuffed it back into his drawer. I figured he wouldn't notice.

My buddy Al—it was his umbrella. Al is my coworker, a 6-foot-4-inch black man. I am a 5-foot-2-inch pasty white woman.

We are practically twins.

But Al is also burly and muscular, very capable-looking, a graphic designer with artsy retro-glasses and close-cropped hair. His look says either "I can design you a logo" or "I can kick your ass," depending on his mood.

Though we work in downtown Columbus, we both hail from greater Youngstown, and we are of the opinion that this makes us savvier—and maybe a little tougher—than most folks. On our breaks, we like to discuss "Youngstown Things."

Youngstown Things are shortcuts in your day, little life hacks of possessions, methods, even attitudes, that can make a difference in your environment and your bank account. Here are some Youngstown Things that my buddy Al and I recommend:

- Ten inches of white stuff and a Level 3 snow emergency? Pffftt. That's a cake-walk for scrappy Mahoning Valley folks. Anyway, it's easier to drive during bad weather in Youngstown—all the potholes are filled with snow. Badass winter driving skills: Youngstown Thing.
- Stuck in traffic near an exit? Switch lanes and pass everyone on the right, then squeeze back over. Sure, you'll piss off some folks, but guess what? You're almost home; they're still in traffic. Passing dummies on the right: totally a Youngstown Thing.
- Muffler hanging, water heater leaking, shoes falling

apart? Those from the Yo don't get rid of things that just need a little love; the metaphorical steel mill could close at any time—you'd better hold on to what you have. Loyalty, innovation and duct tape: these are Youngstown Things.

So, yes. As you can see, Al and I spend a good bit of our free time coming up with such rusty wisdom, and indeed, our shared background, nearly identical looks, and great love of Youngstown Things have made us fast friends.

Years ago, on a rainy evening at quitting time, he heard me cussing, and although swearing at work is not uncommon for me, he asked what was wrong.

"I forgot my umbrella," I said, "and it's pouring outside."

"Come over here," he replied.

Al is not to be disobeyed; see info re: big and burly, above. I walked to his cubicle.

He pulled open his file cabinet. "There's an umbrella in here. You can borrow it any time."

And so I did. Borrowed it that night, the next night, and many other rainy nights over the next several years.

Yeah, I own an umbrella. But if I'm at work, it's in the car—six blocks away, and if I'm in the car, it's at my desk. I always know where my umbrella is: my umbrella is wherever I'm not.

The last time I borrowed Al's umbrella, a few weeks ago, it was raining sideways. No such thing as sideways rain, you say? It's Ohio. It rains however the hell it wants, and often. On this particular evening, the wind kicked up, in a sideways fashion, and blew my buddy Al's umbrella inside out, busting the hinges. Broke it beyond repair.

Soaking wet, I hunched my way through the rest of the trek to the car, where I climbed in and threw Al's now useless umbrella into my backseat. Then, before he arrived at work the next day, I snuck over to his file cabinet and slid its mangled, lifeless body back into the drawer.

Do not judge me. He never used the umbrella, so I didn't think he'd discover it any time soon.

Covering your tracks: it's a Youngstown Thing.

No, I didn't feel guilty—just a bit nervous. The man is mostly a gentle giant. If he's in a certain mood, however, Al has been known to pelt me with stress balls.

Hours, days, weeks went by; he said nothing. Until just now, when I heard him grumble, "Come over here."

Oh, I am busted. I can tell by his voice. But Al is not to be disobeyed, so I walk from my desk to his. There it is—the evidence—right in his lap.

"You broke my umbrella."

"Yeah," I reply, looking down at my feet. "Sorry, about that, Al. It was really windy. You remember that one day? A couple weeks ago?"

"I can't believe you broke my umbrella, and didn't even tell me," he shakes his head, looking down at the tangle of metal and nylon in his lap.

"Yeah. Sorry, Al ..."

With his head tilted like this, I can't read his expression, but he makes his disappointment very clear. I hear our coworkers giggling through the thin cubicle walls.

I return to my desk to await my stress-ball pelting, and sitting there, I think long and hard about my actions. I should have come clean about the crime, should have told him I ruined his umbrella after he's been so nice, lending it to me all these years. At the very least, I really should have told him and then bought him a new one.

Ah, but I didn't.

The afternoon wears on, and Al doesn't come pester me at my desk in his normal fashion. I figure he's pretty mad, and probably devising my punishment—one that involves stress balls.

Around 4:30 p.m., he calls to me again.

"Come over here."

I brace myself. I surely don't want to go. But Al is not to be disobeyed, and I report to his cubicle for my pelting.

"Made you something," he grumbles. He hands me what appears to be left of his umbrella. He's removed the pole, disassembled the ribs and cut a hole in the top. I hold it up.

"It's a poncho," he says. "Now you won't get wet in the rain, since you never have your umbrella."

I poke my head through the top and pull it on. True enough, I look like some fool in a poncho. I certainly won't get wet in the rain.

I learned a lot today, mostly that I should always fess up to my office crimes.

But I also learned that sometimes you'll break someone's umbrella, neglect to tell them, stuff it back in his drawer, and he will turn right around and make you a poncho.

And that is definitely a Youngstown Thing.

# TRAFICANT: THE FOLK HERO ON FILM

*By Eric Murphy*

On the morning of September 24, 2014, my phone buzzed nonstop with news that Jim Traficant had been in a horrible tractor accident on his beloved farm in Mahoning County and was not expected to survive. I've spent more than a decade studying the bombastic former congressman, and the last six years weaving together a feature documentary about his rise to power and fall from grace. It was hard to wrap my head around. How could "Jimbo" die? Folk heroes like Davy Crockett, Daniel Boone, or Paul Bunyan aren't supposed to die.

My first Traficant memories take place at my grandmother's house on the west side of Warren. Snippets of the adult conversations often included mentions of Jesus Christ, JFK, and Jim Traficant—and not necessarily in that order. He was the football star turned *Walking Tall* sheriff, and finally he became our Congressman. I was told he stood up for the "little guy." My grandfather worked 41 years at Republic Steel in Warren. When the mills collapsed, he got a $67 a month F.U. until he passed away. Traficant represented my family's hopes, fears, and anger.

A few years later, I got a paper route and began each day scanning the front page of the *Warren Tribune* for a Traficant picture or headline. Most days he was right there on A1. I would later understand that's where he thrived, in the spotlight. Even at a young age, especially at a young age, the guy's entire act really amused me: the polyester suits, the dead animal hair, the vulgar language, the adolescent humor that usually included references to his crotch. I didn't know or really even care about politics, but this guy was fantastic. He cracked me up. On Sundays, I remember lying belly down on my grandmother's green shag carpet just a few feet from the wooden box television, watching Traficant yell directly into the camera. He was looking me in the eyes, like an oddly magnetic WWF wrestler.

I attended Youngstown State in the late '90s, when the area was a really bleak place. Those years almost play like a black-and-white movie in my memory. Mobsters were killing each other on city streets at high-noon. An honest prosecutor was shot a few days before Christmas. The violence was shocking and pervasive. Nightly, a parade of wannabe wiseguys, political scumbags, and drug dealers led the evening news—it was routine to see disgraced elected officials in handcuffs. This is when everything came into focus for me; the charming folklore of mobsters and politicians now had a bloody, brutal reality. Perhaps not coincidentally, this was also the same time I knew I had to become a filmmaker. I wanted to understand the history of the Mahoning Valley—the collapse of the mills, the role of the mob, and how our checkered past was destroying our tenuous future.

After graduation, armed with equal parts frustration and idealism, I volunteered on Tim Ryan's grassroots campaign for the Ohio Senate. We had a small ragtag group of kids and a few retirees—and I just loved it. Tim Ryan was 26, lived at home, and had one off-the-rack suit, but most importantly to me, he had some amazing stories from his days as Traficant's aide and driver. Those stories made me feel like I was riding shotgun with them. Tim regaled me with fascinating tales that illuminated Traficant's charisma and eccentric behavior, including his demands to keep the car windows rolled up, even on the most beautiful summer evenings. In retrospect, he probably didn't want that mop-top wig blowing in the wind.

I remember the first time I saw Traficant in person, it was at the Trumbull Country Democratic endorsement at DiVieste's in Warren. He arrived very late, moments before it was his turn to speak, clad in a black fleece pullover, sans his typical shitty suit. He made a grand entrance, slapping politicos on the side of the neck with his 25-pound right hand. Everyone stopped. He was like a movie star.

My experience working on Tim's campaign ignited my obsession with this material. I realized this was *my* story to tell. And with a chip on my shoulder and less than 1,000 bucks to my name, I moved to Los Angeles to pursue a career in filmmaking. While attending graduate school at Loyola Marymount, I based my student film loosely on Tim's campaign and Ed O'Neill agreed to play a Traficant-esque character—the mentor to the young idealist protégé. That short film turned into a feature screenplay that eventually led to my documentary. We began filming in 2009 when Traficant was released from prison and finished in 2015.

In making the film, I pored through every court document, devoured every C-SPAN clip, and pursued anything that could help me understand Traficant and his relationship to the Mahoning Valley. My opinion swayed almost daily. How could the same person be both devastatingly brilliant and bat-shit crazy? I kept asking myself: Was Traficant a transcendent hero who spoke truth to power? Or, was he Youngstown's cautionary tale of greed, corruption, and ego? No matter how galvanized my opinions became over the years, I decided to present a portrait of Traficant as a real person—the good, the bad, and the utterly inexplicable. Much like the blast furnaces that dominated the landscape and our psyche for generations, Traficant was vibrant and powerful, but he became a relic of a bygone era. A fading symbol of what Youngstown once was.

My childhood fascination with an enigmatic character turned into a filmmaking odyssey, one where memories and emotions are confronted with facts and truth—and folk heroes are revealed as deeply flawed. As I write this, I'm putting the finishing touches on the film, *TRAFICANT: The Congressman of Crimetown*, with great anticipation of our premiere at the Cleveland International Film Festival. It's been a long journey from my grandmother's house to Los Angeles and back home again.

*Los Angeles*
*February 2015*

# IN THE CENTURY OF RUST

the city's shoulders glittered with fiery dust.
Dramatic, wind-driven, it cloaked every citizen,
and found its way into each
of the body's hollows. It fell

from their mouths in scabs
when they sang too loud, yawned too long
or sighed too heavily. It left

iron orange streaks on their tongues
when they kissed, so it was always apparent
when two had been kissing. They had to

brush their hands along each other's spines
each night just to keep their backs

from rusting out—*that stuff,*
mothers would say to one another,
*will eat through anything.*

*Rochelle Hurt,* from *The Rusted City*

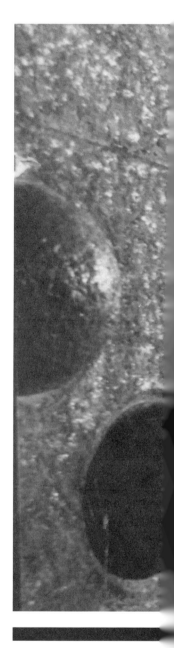

For most of the 20th century, the blast furnaces at
Youngstown Sheet & Tube stood as sentinels over
the city that relied upon them for its livelihood.
*Tom Wood*

# ICE AGE PROPHECIES AND THE DEAD KILLER

*By Tom Wood*

n 1997, I traded my Youngstown steel for Rocky Mountain stone. I now live in the far-off, mystical land of Colorado, where the mountains are tall and the grass is greener—literally. I am paid to get high at work, but probably not in the way that most folks would imagine most Coloradans accomplish that feat these days. I am employed to teach cell tower climbers, wind turbine technicians, and bridge inspectors how not to die and how to rescue each other. I also spend a lot of time volunteering with a mountain rescue team, searching for, rescuing, and sometimes recovering folks who've had a bad day in the mountains.

But whether I am 200 feet in the air on a cell tower teaching safe-climbing techniques or volunteering my time alongside my fellow Colorado mountain rescuers to recover the body of a fallen hiker from the side of a mountain, I am still of Youngstown. Every now and then, something—like the smell of death—reminds me of that.

In the early '60s, instead of running to the mountains, my grandparents found themselves fleeing them. The desperate pursuit of the American dream drove them (via the Hillbilly Highway) away from the greedy clutches of the coal barons and their company stores in a little-too-wild, not-so wonderful West Virginia to the bustling streets of Youngstown. Known as "Preacher Click," my grandfather Glenneth Click was a moonshiner turned Southern Freewill Baptist Preacher who had worked in the mines from the age of 13. After relocating his family of seven to Ohio, he devoted more than two decades of his life to the care and feeding of Sweet Jenny at Youngstown Sheet & Tube. As reward for his dedicated service, Jenny took three of the toes on his right foot. They were blown out the end of his boot like toothpaste shot out of a tube when a piece of steel was dropped from a malfunctioning overhead crane onto his steel-toed boots. A lifetime of hard work finally caught up with him in early 1977 when his black lungs and failing heart forced him into retirement.

Later that same year, when the blast furnace fires died on Black Monday, there was still a lot of metal to be had in the Mahoning Valley. It just had to be harvested from the businesses that died alongside the mills at Brier Hill, Struthers, and McDonald. The enormous steel carcass of Youngstown was ripe for the picking. In the mid-80s, during the summer of my junior year at Niles McKinley High School, I was one of the scores of human flies employed to help pick it clean. I worked my first summer job at a place I'll call Heaton Amalgamated.

Heaton Amalgamated occupied two or three city blocks. A bulging chain link fence ringed its perimeter and barely held the random scraps of rusty metal that threatened to spill over the top.

Just walking by it made you want to get a tetanus shot.

Long before I became a mountain rescuer in Colorado, I performed my first body recovery while working with my pal Will Pfeifer (the only person in this story whose name has not been changed). Will would later go on to become an accomplished comic book writer, but on a particularly memorable, sweltering August day, he and I were just two scrawny kids hired as laborers tasked with moving piles of scrap metal to be sorted, sandblasted, painted, or recycled.

Normally, we were aided by Virgil, the yard's painter and heavy equipment operator. Virgil looked a lot like the white-trash version of the Wild Man from Borneo. There was a space between his two front teeth wide enough to drive a Buick through. The bushy, jet-black hair on his head, heavily bearded face, and always-exposed chest was permanently frosted with over-sprayed orange paint from the high-powered spray rig he used to rustproof the metal (sprayed on liberally and without a respirator, thereby ensuring that the microscopic hairs lining his lungs matched the exposed hair on the rest of him).

That paint was so toxic and noxious that it either killed or stoned every living thing within a 200-foot radius of his work area.

In fact, Virgil's affinity for paint fumes may have contributed to his spontaneous combustion a few weeks earlier during a Fourth of July barbecue when he unwisely tried to ignite his charcoal grill with a half-gallon of gasoline instead of lighter fluid. The resulting fireball landed him in the burn unit.

So we were without Virgil's heavy equipment expertise and his eau-de-Sherwin-Williams cologne on that particularly hot summer post-Fourth of July afternoon when yard boss Ralph approached us with an assignment.

Ralph was cool and endearingly odd.

He sagely (and often) predicted that another Ice Age was nigh. He reminded us of his prognostic prowess most often over lunch each day. He was seriously worried that the next Ice Age would swoop in like an unannounced storm and wipe out humanity as we knew it.

"See if I'm not right," he would say to us, his mouth full of bologna sandwich and his eyes freakishly huge behind thick glasses. His wiry gray hair was streaked with a few remaining strands of black and stood at kinky attention—much like the abused wire brushes we used to scrape rust spots—as he sipped coffee from the red plastic cup that topped his plaid Thermos.

"You ever see the looks on the faces of those cavemen frozen in blocks of ice? They looked surprised!" he would say.

But on this particular day, Ralph had more mundane matters on his mind.

"Why don't you boys clear up that big pile of scrap steel shelving back there in the corner of the yard?" Ralph asked us in his nasal voice as we finished our lunches. The aforementioned pile was as tall as the Great Pyramid at Giza and seemed to be just as meticulously constructed.

But at least the pile was in the back of the yard, away from the eagle eyes of Rueben, the ass-kissing blowhard who went to Will's church. Rueben enjoyed ordering us around and then regaling Will's parents with tales of all the great life lessons we were learning by moving rusty pieces of metal from point A to point B and then back again.

Halfway through our task, Will and I found a body.

It was the first time I experienced the smell of rotting flesh.

The body was that of the missing Killer.

Killer was the resident junkyard dog that disappeared in early June. Not much remained of that enormous German shepherd (now renamed "Killed" by Will and I). There was a spiked collar and soupy pile of fur and bones—that was about it. After relaying the news of our find to Rueben (now not-so-jokingly renamed "Asshole" by Will and me), he charged us with scooping up the remains in a shovel and hurling them over the fence and into the Mahoning River on the other side—without hurling our lunch onto his boots as he stood watch over our efforts. Though it was difficult to choke back the bile, we were successful on both accounts, but only barely. The cloying, sweet-sick smell of death clung to the tiny hairs in my nostrils and the taste of rot hung in the back of my throat for days.

Who would have ever suspected that the only skill I salvaged from my time at Heaton Amalgamated would be an aptitude for dealing with death and decay? A skill that would, two decades later, serve me so well as a non-paid professional mountain rescuer in Colorado.

So though I wouldn't list having a cast-iron gag reflex as a marketable skill on my resume, it has come in handy more than a few dozen times on the body recoveries I've helped our Colorado-based mountain rescue team perform. To this very day, the earthy scent of death catapults me straight back to Killer, that dead junkyard dog. Straight back to Youngstown.

## GHOST LUNCHBOX

*24" x 24" relief print*
*graphite and black ink on canvas*

My father brought home a lot of ghost stories from the mill, everything from ghost trains to hooded figures. My favorite is a story that happened while the men were all at lunch.

As my dad tells it, the men were all on break and sitting down eating their lunch when one of the cranes began to operate. It wasn't just a slight movement or shifting of a gear—someone or something began doing the job. The "ghost" worked for a minute and then stopped. There was nobody running the crane.

"Ghost Lunchbox" is an imagined artifact from this story. –Rob Hudak

# WHY I STAYED

*By Mike Ray*

About 15 years ago, I was talking with a family friend, a prominent member of the community. He asked me, "Do you know what Youngstown's number one export is?"

I racked my brain. The steel mills and allied industries had been gone for years. Cars? The General Motors plant in Lordstown was still working around the clock, and the idea of GM going bankrupt was as far-fetched as a phone that could take pictures.

"People," he said—and he was right.

My memories start in the days after what is still called Black Monday, when Youngstown Sheet & Tube started its slide toward oblivion. It's really the line of demarcation in the history of Youngstown and the Mahoning Valley. The people old enough to remember the days before it talked of fat pay envelopes, home ownership, and a city that had been booming since the early days of the 20th century.

The people who aren't old enough to remember the good old days? Well, you won't find a lot of them in the area. In fact, some people saw the mills closing as the first step of the "brain drain" they're afraid of in Ohio, coming up with the slogan "Keep the 'Young' in Youngstown."

It's very easy to get hung up on the people who left because there are a lot of them. And so what do we talk about instead? The mob? High school football? The good old days before Black Monday?

In fact, the overarching question in the Mahoning Valley over the past 25 years is "Why are you here?" The people who stayed ask it to anyone who happens to relocate here, disbelieving that anyone would willingly move to a town that—sometimes deservedly—has gotten no end of bad press.

It's a question I've been asked myself. I graduated from Youngstown State—my sister and I are the first ones in our family to go to college—and took a job that required a certain amount of travel. I saw a lot of places throughout the Midwest, but it never entered my mind that I would live anywhere other than Youngstown. And when I say Youngstown, I mean the city. One of the funny things about any city is the number of people who claim it, the people who say "Cleveland" instead of "Brecksville," or the people who say "Youngstown" instead of "Boardman."

And when I returned to Youngstown, it had never occurred to me that I wouldn't be involved in trying to make it a better place. I was active in high school. I was active on campus at YSU. There was never any doubt I'd be active in the community. My story's not special. There are plenty of other people who are doing their jobs but aren't satisfied just doing that. They try to make the community better.

In 1984, Mike Kovach was one of the unemployed in the Mahoning Valley. For most of his life, he had the kind of success story the area—and the entire country—was proud to share. He went from cleaning parts in an Andrews Avenue industrial shop at 16 to being the shop foreman and an undergraduate engineering student at YSU two years later. At 18, he became the plant manager. He had attracted attention and offers from other companies but remained committed to his employer in the kind of blue-collar loyalty Youngstown inculcates. He offered to buy the company—and that's why he was unemployed. Such effrontery was not well received, and he was fired.

He didn't remain unemployed for long, and in 18 months, he'd taken out a second mortgage and used his savings to open City Machine Technologies on Aug. 9, 1985—down the street from his former employer.

1985 wasn't a good year for the Mahoning Valley. Unemployment continued to hover around 12 percent. Efforts to lure GM's Saturn plant were unsuccessful, and the blimp factory didn't pan out either. At the end of May, a series of tornadoes ripped through the Mahoning Valley. It wasn't the best climate for a new business.

It was a leap of faith for Mike but also a smart decision. Youngstown was home, and on a more pragmatic level, he had business connections in the area. The company opened a second location on Rayen Avenue, and then a third on Martin Luther King Jr. Boulevard. The company now employs more than 75 people, with more than half having been with the company for at least 10 years. There's that loyalty again.

Despite offers from investors and equity groups, the family still owns the company and runs it. And that's why Mike thinks it's still successful. He still comes to the Andrews Avenue office every day to make sure the work's being done.

He also checks on the neighborhood. A neighborhood cleanup led to the Andrews Avenue Industrial Parkway, which forms partnerships with YSU and the city, leading to improvements like landscaping and signage.

Also in 1985, Augie DiRusso bought the old Berkowitz Fish on Rayen Avenue. He was going to make sausage there. With the new facility, they would qualify for U.S. Department of Agriculture inspection, which means the sausage could be sold across state lines.

Twenty-one years earlier, Augie started making sausage at the family grocery store in Lowellville. He enlisted his relatives, including his nephew Robert. At 12, Robert was selling sausage in the family's concession trailer at local festivals and fairs. By high school, he had his own concession route, with 19 stops, and he continued with the route while he pursued an accounting degree from Youngstown State University in the late 1970s, as millworkers were undergoing retraining and fighting for their existence.

By 1990, Robert was helping run the family business, and in 1993, he bought the company from his uncle. The Riverbend Industrial Park, the area on Rayen Avenue that held so much promise a decade earlier for the business, was starting to decline. Businesses drifted away to the suburbs, and the vacant buildings created a welcoming atmosphere for criminal activity.

Local businesses—including Dominion East Ohio, Gulu Electrical Contractors, Carney Plastics and Mike Kovach's City Machine Technologies—started to clean up the area, spurring the formation of the Riverbend Business Park Association. Robert took a leadership role, and the area is cleaner and safer than it was before, with break-ins declining and the blighted buildings being demolished.

The improvements at the business park also made it conducive for expansion. In 2000, the company started selling its products in stores, including Sam's Club. A box storage room was added in 2003, the shipping and receiving area got a new dock in 2005 and the next year, the production room was expanded with the installation of a blast freezer. In 2012, DiRusso's Sausage bought 1.5 acres for expansion, bringing the concession trailers that were stored and maintained previously in the suburbs. DiRusso's now has five acres in the business park and is working on buying more land.

Robert never considered being one of those businesses that decamped for the suburbs. The location was attractive, near highways and with signage visible from high-traffic areas, so he dug in his heels and made the area around it better.

Every Youngstown expatriate has his or her favorite food, the one restaurant they have to stop at when they come home. Several of the local pizza places have their own following—some even will ship their products. For others, it's Handel's ice cream. For me, it's DiRusso's sausage. It's a staple at my house parties, and I'll bring it with me to others. When a group of my high school friends—many of them no longer living in Youngstown—gathered in Baltimore for the Ohio State/Navy game, we made DiRusso's sausage in the tailgate lot.

"Why are you here?" shouldn't be a routine question. It shouldn't even be a conversation starter. It needs to be a challenge. "Why are you here?" should be shorthand for "What is your purpose, and are you doing what you should be doing right now?"

# CROSSING THE CENTER STREET BRIDGE

*By Andrea Wood*

The day I started my career in journalism, Sept. 9, 1974, the drive from my apartment to WYTV Channel 33 took me across the Center Street Bridge that spanned Republic Steel's mill. It was exciting to see the orange clouds of smoke, billowing steam, and yellow-hot sparks flaring below as the steel was poured and shaped. There was Youngstown's passion—its lifeblood.

Not long after that day, an entrance to the Youngstown Sheet & Tube Campbell Works filled with steelworkers pumping their fists and shouting, "Strike! Strike! Strike!" When my cameraman turned on his portable light to film the midnight walkout, the steelworkers' energy electrified me. I waved my arms and shouted, "Louder, louder!" The next day plant security notified the TV station's general manager that I had crossed the line.

It was easy to do.

In Youngstown, lines were always blurring. If a stoplight took too long to change and no one was coming the other way, it was OK to drive through the light. If a six-piece set of Corning Ware cookware fell off a train at the rail yards, a friend of a friend said three fives paid bragging rights for the bargain.

Fencing stolen goods, gambling, prostitution, loan-sharking, and extortion—all were happening here. Organized crime was accepted in this tough-as-steel culture, rationalized as victimless even as Cleveland and Pittsburgh crime families bombed and killed each other for decades while they fought for control of the territory, its rackets, certain labor unions, and police departments.

The long-accepted explanation dates to the arrival of immigrants from Italy and Eastern Europe at the beginning of the 20th century— the Black Hand and the other shadow-government traditions they brought with them. But this gives everyone else a free pass, including the industry barons, who profited greatly and looked the other way. My father, who owned a small company in Pittsburgh that sold industrial parts, told me that to get a big order from Sheet & Tube, word was you had to pay off someone in the purchasing department.

When I moved to Youngstown in September 1974, Richard Nixon had just been pardoned and Woodward and Bernstein's investigative journalism was the standard to which I aspired. In Youngstown, nightshift cops had just been caught breaking into appliance stores and loading washers and dryers onto trucks. A few days before the police burglary ring was exposed, 21-year-old John Robek, on the Youngtown Police Department payroll as a drug informant, went hunting with another informant and never returned. A headless torso turned up floating in a body of water not far from the woods that Robek was last seen entering. The Mahoning County coroner, at the request of the sheriff's department, quickly cremated the body, leaving Robek's parents to wonder, for the rest of their lives, if that was their son.

During the 1970s, a series of drug-related killings took the lives of middlemen as a veteran thug and burglar, then a heroin supplier, and those he commanded strengthened their hold on the pipeline and dirty cops. In October 1974, when the thug-turned-drug boss settled an old score, his junkie son and friends were ordered to bury the body. Two months later, a 21-year-old woman, Joanne Coughlin, turned up at the wrong party at the wrong time in the apartment of one of those loose-lipped junkies. Two days after Christmas 1974, Joanne and her car disappeared, leaving her parents to wonder, for the rest of their lives, what happened to their daughter.

These were the stories I was determined to investigate—naively confident justice would one day prevail—and as I did, Youngstown's organized crime and public corruption culture was revealed to me in all its brutal reality. The fiction of *The Godfather*, deceptive in its Hollywood glamour, only added to the perverse pride residents took in the city's nicknames—"Little Chicago," when gambling parlors ran wide-open in the 1930s and 1940s, then "Bombtown" and "Murdertown USA" in the 1960s when mob killings drew the attention of the *Saturday Evening Post* and other national news organizations. The sick underbelly of this steel town was never concealed. But until the mills closed, there was no carcass to pick dry.

Then everyone said they saw it coming.

By the 1970s, steelworkers were complaining that equipment had not been maintained and promised furnace upgrades were never made. Labor and management, intransigent foes in nearly everything else, warned that EPA regulations threatened everyone's livelihood. On Sept. 19, 1977, when Lykes Brothers, the New Orleans shipbuilding company that had bought Sheet & Tube, announced the closing of the Campbell Works, the immediate toll was 5,000 jobs. By the time the last domino fell, 50,000 steel and related industry jobs had evaporated in the Mahoning Valley, and Youngstown was Exhibit A in the deindustrialization of the Rust Belt, a city full of camera-ready images that illustrated severe socio-economic fallout.

It's difficult to identify the first vultures to circle the ruins; there were so many. Among them, outsiders who promised thousands of new jobs from a blimp factory (once government funds were secured to build and operate the plant), two separate airplane factory projects (same government funding requirements), a brewery and a specialty car manufacturer. All were pie in the sky.

Who knows if the politicians knew all along that the vultures' big, quick-fix promises were ludicrous. Jim Traficant, the most charismatic and astute of them all, resurrected the lake-to-river canal project as one of his job-creation miracles. Variations of the canal, conceived to reduce costs for transporting minerals needed to make steel, were proposed as early as the 1920s. None got beyond the talking stage.

In the early 1980s, as unemployment benefits ran out and people began to lose their homes, the public's attitude alternated between depression and clinging to hope for a savior to descend—a role Traficant executed to perfection, exploiting the anger and frustration of a constituency that believed it was the victim of Big Business and indifferent government.

Each Sunday the daily newspaper recycled a death-of-steel story or retold a chapter from the industry's heydays. The exodus from the Mahoning Valley was well underway. Commercial and residential arsons for profit became routine. Those who still drove across a deteriorating Center Street Bridge saw darkness where yellow molten steel once lit the night.

For me, opportunity intervened and my career took a new route, away from television news and the nightly slaughter reports—both economic and criminal—that headlined the newscasts I anchored. In August 1984, a friend, Ralph Zerbonia, and I launched the *Youngstown Business Journal*. Clueless about the entrepreneurial challenges we would face, we vowed to create a new business narrative to counter the doom-and-gloom.

It's as amazing to me that *The Business Journal* survived, as it must be to those who were sure we would fail. We should have. And we would have failed were it not for those who believed in the mission we adopted—to tell positive stories about homegrown businesses determined to stay here and rebuild, one job at a time. As we rooted for these companies, reporting what they made, the markets they served and the perseverance of their leaders, they rooted for us. So did four investors, including my father, none of whom ever saw a return on their investment other than an alternative voice.

Did we put blinders on? You bet. As others chronicled the fallout from the shutdowns, we reported on the entrepreneurial ingenuity that remained and drew strength from faith, family values, and sound business practices. But we drew the line when it came to the business vultures. In the edition heralding the *Youngstown Business Journal's* first anniversary, the front-page headline reported, "Tall Tales Surround Developer." The story outlined the background of a newly arrived promoter whose job-creation promises had played the circuit of depressed industrial towns elsewhere.

Then there was the Phar-Mor debacle, a homegrown discount drugstore chain that Sam Walton once described as the stiffest competition for his Walmart. Phar-Mor, bankrolled by Pittsburgh's

Giant Eagle grocery chain, made its headquarters in the old Strouss' department store in downtown Youngstown. The company changed the name of the building to the Phar-Mor Center and created hundreds of jobs in the Mahoning Valley. It also created the World Basketball League and fielded one of its teams, the Youngstown Pride.

On July 30, 1992, while trumpeting its success at a press event in Ashtabula, Phar-Mor opened its 300th store at that city's new mall. Five days later, the corporation accused its co-founder, Mickey Monus, and chief financial officer, Patrick Finn, of embezzlement and cooking the books to show $350 million in phony profits. By the time Monus went to trial in 1994, federal prosecutors claimed the fraud and embezzlement added up to $1.1 billion, at the time the largest corporate fraud in United States history (today small potatoes).

Phar-Mor filed Chapter 11 bankruptcy in 1992, reorganized under court protection three years later, and filed bankruptcy again in 2001, this time after a Dallas holding company bled it dry. Today the company and its stores are only a memory.

There were other vultures—and still are—but *The Business Journal* has covered many more heroes over the last 30 years, men and women who put their shovels in the ground and turned over dirt to build anew. Not the least of these heroes were the federal agents and prosecutors who dug up the roots of public corruption in the 1990s and sent a truckload of judges, county commissioners, police officers, prosecutors, gangsters—and eventually Congressman Traficant—to prison.

Regional economic development agencies and community improvement corporations were formed, conduits for government and bank financing were established, government grants were sought for the remediation of industrial brownfields (a process that continues today), industrial parks were created, and abandoned land was sold for $1 to companies willing to build in Youngstown and create jobs.

By the 1990s, business leaders had coalesced behind the recognition that political turf wars worked against the region as a whole. Chambers of commerce in Youngstown, Warren, and Niles merged to form a regional chamber that took the lead in coordinating economic development incentives. Priorities were agreed upon to maximize state and federal funds for infrastructure improvements in Mahoning and Trumbull counties. New business, political, and labor leadership took hold.

In 2002, Tim Ryan, once an intern in Traficant's office, won the election for the expelled congressman's vacant seat and, at age 29, began building alliances and seniority to secure strategic appropriations for development and educational initiatives. Truth be told, Traficant did bring home some bacon—most notably the first $26.8 million to build the downtown municipal arena today known as the Covelli Centre—but his greed and ego led him to squander tremendous political talents and instead perpetrate the national image of a community represented by a clown.

As Ryan came on the scene, another native son, Jay Williams, began planning for how Youngstown neighborhoods could be preserved in a shrinking city. After overseeing the Youngstown 2010 plan, Williams was elected mayor as an independent with widespread support from faith-based groups and suburban Republicans.

Organized labor did its part as well. Management and union leadership at the General Motors manufacturing complex in Lordstown, the poster plant for labor unrest in the 1970s, learned one of the lessons from the steel shutdowns and rebuilt a plant culture based on mutual respect, collaboration, and cooperation. Community campaigns sponsored by business supported the autoworkers in securing new products for their assembly line. Today the plant turns out General Motors Co.'s No. 1 passenger car, the Cruze.

Then there is the remarkable story of Vallourec, the pipe and steel plants that straddle Youngstown and the city of Girard on the site of the old Sheet & Tube Brier Hill Works. The survival of this plant, through many iterations as various operators struggled to keep the original mill producing steel, and subsequent construction of a $1 billion pipe mill adjacent to it, is a contemporary source of pride in the Mahoning Valley's steel heritage.

The high-tech pipe mill opened in 2012, the result of considerable investment by its French parent company, as well as the federal, state and local governments. An $81 million threading mill quickly followed and today Vallourec employs more than 400 highly skilled steelworkers at its Youngstown operations. In four elections, workers there rejected representation by organized labor.

Vallourec's new pipe mill supplies the oil and gas industry, and by 2012 exploration of Utica and Marcellus shales fueled hope that the region's mineral deposits would lead to another boom, just like natural resources brought the iron and steel mills here more than 100 years ago.

But the people and businesses that stayed here through the steel shutdowns were the ones who created the can-do spirit, the belief that we could shape our destiny. Give us a hand, sure, but also believe in us.

Looking back, the Ecumenical Coalition of the Mahoning Valley, born within days of the Campbell Works shutdown, embodied the elements it would take to overcome the catastrophe. While the coalition failed in its two-year, $300 million-plus attempt to buy the shuttered mill and operate it as a community-worker cooperative, it embodied the core values of faith, family, and confidence in our ability to rebuild.

True, Youngstown's poverty rate remains staggering and its school system dysfunctional. The city's high income tax still gives reason for businesses to flee, the racial divide persists, and violent crime discourages renewal. The blinders are not on to these serious structural impediments to community prosperity, nor to those who perpetuate public corruption. Still, the people of the Mahoning Valley are digging out.

One job at a time, small businesses are doing their part.

One grant at a time, charitable foundations are funding neighborhood and educational programs.

One community garden at a time, inner-city residents are harvesting grassroots pride.

One startup at a time, the Youngstown Business Incubator is nurturing software developers and earning international recognition.

One future leader at a time, Youngstown State University is educating the next generation of entrepreneurs and teachers, expanding its campus toward downtown. Homegrown developers are converting landmark buildings into student housing, small retail and nightlife venues, and the central city is finding new life as young adults see opportunity in a Mahoning Valley where their grandparents lost theirs.

A mural that depicts musicians enjoying the downtown entertainment scene greets drivers as they head north to the Market Street bridge into downtown. On the opposite side of the street is a vacant building with graffiti in big block letters: "WE ARE A GENERATION!"

On the eastern edge of the city, the Center Street Bridge, rebuilt after the old Republic Steel property was cleared, today crosses a remediated brownfield fronted by an auto body shop, a company that sells aggregates and a convenience store. A dilapidated vacant building that stands at the bridge's southwest edge, a former steelworkers bar where gambling and prostitution were rife decades ago, declares the identical affirmation, "WE ARE A GENERATION!"

We have come full circle.

In the late 1970s, steel mills were closing and workers were losing their jobs. A group of steelworkers from Youngstown went to US Steel headquarters in Pittsburgh to protest. Being from the Youngstown area, I wanted to be there and capture what I could. The group of protesters started outside. Security let them inside the building but wouldn't let them pass beyond the lobby. I thought this image summed up the event and the worries of the protesters—members of a proud steel town feeling like everything they worked for was slipping away, and there wasn't much they could do to stop it. *Mark Moretti*

Nearly a decade after Youngstown Sheet & Tube closed its doors on Black Monday, artifacts from that day remained where they were left by the workers as they clocked out. ***Tom Wood***

A stark view from inside the abandoned Wick Building is framed by the Home Savings Building, at left, and the Mahoning County Jail, at right. Long vacant, the Wick Building is currently undergoing renovation. *Sean Posey*

RISE

# DEFENDING YOUNGSTOWN

*By Phil Kidd*

I returned to Youngstown in the summer of 2004. I had no job and nowhere to live. I came back because I missed Youngstown, because I wanted to make it a better place.

I had spent several years as an undergraduate at Youngstown State University around the dawn of the new millennium. However, interest and opportunity eventually took me elsewhere, like they had for so many others. In my case, it was the military.

While I was stationed in the middle of Kansas, I followed city happenings through online articles, videos, and websites. At the time, the city was going through an elaborate planning process called "Youngstown 2010." From what I could tell, it appeared to be a serious effort that was generating a great deal of community energy.

During this same time period, the book *Steeltown U.S.A.* had been published by two YSU professors, Sherry Lee Linkon and John Russo. It was a compelling account of not only the history of the city but also its class and cultural context.

It was the combination of the plan and the book that eventually prompted me to return to Youngstown and find a way to get involved. So, in the summer of 2004, I landed in Wick Park, a historic district on the city's near-north side whose prime had long since passed. The neighborhood was anchored by a 34-acre forest-like park, which provided the neighborhood its namesake.

The park itself was bordered by four churches of various denominations and an incredible concert hall built in the 1920s. Its acoustic qualities have been compared to Carnegie Hall by those who have played both.

The homes—those which remained—were once home to many of Youngstown's elite: steel barons, bankers, doctors, and even notable individuals such as Civil War-era Ohio Governor David Tod and John D. "Bonesetter" Reese, who some consider the godfather of physical therapy in professional athletics.

Much of the neighborhood's architecture was that of prominent early 20th century design. However, in the 21st century, much of the neighborhood could have passed as the setting for a Cormac McCarthy novel.

Having no plan, I lived out the back of my truck near the park for about a week until finding an apartment in a building that also served as the headquarters of the neighborhood's fledgling development corporation.

"This place is rough but we can work out a good deal if you can help me fix it up," the organization's director said.

The space was totaled: dog feces on the shag carpet, peeling paint on the walls, sticky cabinets and old food caked to the stove top, unsealed windows. You name it. Whoever last lived here left in a hurry and didn't care much about the place when they did.

I did the best I could to make it functional. The director was satisfied. However, he and what remained of the staff would soon vacate the building without any notification. By default, I joined the ranks of the squatters.

The only other person living in the building was a former star YSU football player from the 1970s who had at one point earned a pro tryout, a master's degree, and always loved Wick Park for workouts (which he still did daily).

We became good friends and for the better part of a year, we warded off scrappers who threw pebbles at windows in the middle of the night to see if the building was occupied, kept riffraff from hanging out on the corner, picked up trash in the park, and maintained our yard, as well as the one next door.

We did the best we could. However, maintenance issues eventually became greater than what we could manage on our own, so we moved on. My escrowed rent would later be invested into evening graduate school classes at YSU.

---

People are always surprised to learn that I am not from

Youngstown. I am from Burgettstown, PA, where my father spent nearly 20 years working for the Redevelopment Authority of Washington County and was very involved in the community.

However, he suffered from severe depression over the last several years of his life and died of a heart attack at 39. I was 15 at the time, and his death left me with a lot of anger, often misdirected, but eventually channeled into civic activism later in life.

My mother worked in affordable housing for the county and state. And my grandfather and uncle—two other major influences in my life—worked at Weirton Steel, about an hour south of Youngstown along the Ohio River in the West Virginia panhandle.

This was my DNA. So, my bond with Youngstown felt like I was following a genetic imperative.

In my view, Youngstown was a bellwether for other older industrial cities—those that serve as the rivets that hold the proverbial Rust Belt together. These were the types of communities that provided opportunity for my family and helped shaped me as a person. Working to ensure their survival was like working to ensure the survival of my own heritage.

Eventually, the "Youngstown 2010 Plan" was completed after years of community input and high expectations. National media, as well as planning groups, heralded it as a bold new vision for a struggling, older industrial city.

A young city planner by the name of Jay Williams who helped facilitate the planning process decided to run for mayor as an independent the following year. I joined his grassroots campaign and was introduced to the city by way of thousands of door fronts.

It was an important experience that would greatly affect my decision to stay in Youngstown. During the campaign, I met many folks who helped me better understand the history and dynamics of the community. I also met other idealistic newcomers like myself who were excited about the possibility of change in a community where progress had seemed to go to die for nearly three decades.

Black. White. Old. Young. City. Suburbs. There were many people involved in the campaign. It was highly charged and invigorating.

Williams would go on to win convincingly in what local political experts considered an upset. In doing so, he became the city's first African-American mayor, its youngest, and the first independent in more than 80 years.

My first venture into civic participation in Youngstown had resulted in a historic campaign that had been followed by the launch of a highly regarded new plan for the city. It was an exciting time to be in Youngstown.

---

Inspired by Youngstown 2010 and Williams's win, I wanted to contribute something of my own to the effort. As someone not from Youngstown, I felt that the prevailing self-deprecating attitude of the area—while perhaps justified to some degree—was something that had to be overcome. Maybe someone not born and raised in Youngstown could get folks to begin to see the potential once again.

So this was the battle I chose and my weapon of choice was a single slogan: Defend Youngstown.

There were other defend/city slogans elsewhere which had their own meanings, and I felt it would work in Youngstown, too. It was edgy and got right to the point, and that's the language Youngstown speaks.

My interpretation of Defend Youngstown was this: acknowledge the past. Be realistic about the challenges of the present. Get informed and involved if you want to change the trajectory of the future. It was now or never.

I didn't know the best way to go about this so I took to the streets. More specifically, I stood in the middle of downtown with a sign that said "Defend Youngstown" until folks would approach me. This, of course, got people's attention. While some felt I was naïve and foolish (which I probably was), others were just as passionate and supported my effort. I learned a lot in those conversations. And some of it was organizational.

One gentleman told me he liked the message and enthusiasm

but that I was wasting my time standing downtown. I needed to get organized if I wanted to spread the idea.

So Defend Youngstown eventually became a blog and a T-shirt concept (and later an avant-garde gift shop and community information center called Youngstown Nation).

As social media tools like Facebook and Twitter began to emerge, so did a growing network of folks who were interested in the city once again by way of Defend.

In 2008, while finishing my graduate degree and considering law school, I was encouraged to apply for the position of downtown events and marketing director with the City of Youngstown.

While not knowing much about event planning or marketing, I did have an idea of what type of events the community wanted to see based on years of conversations with patrons. And Defend Youngstown was becoming an informal marketing campaign of sorts itself. Maybe I could do this?

So I applied and was offered the job.

Being new to city government, the learning curve was somewhat steep initially, but I eventually figured things out. I scratched out a budget with City Council, figured out the permits needed to make things happen and, in some cases, enlisted friends to help with the events themselves. The most memorable experience was the manual construction of a gigantic, wooden movie screen days before the launch of the new outdoor movie series.

Fortunately, the events were successful and brought thousands upon thousands of people back to the downtown area—many of whom were new to the city or hadn't been downtown in years. During this same period of time, a prominent local foundation had just completed a plan that would almost totally reform the way in which they directed their giving.

Inspired in part by Youngstown 2010 and realizing more capacity was needed to make actual progress, the foundation decided to shift their focus almost entirely to the inner cities of Youngstown and Warren.

One of the initiatives born from this shift was the creation of an organization dedicated to helping residents organize and find solutions to local issues. The group had developed a campaign around the vacant or blighted properties in which I volunteered my time to help rate.

Eventually, I was offered a job to help lead this campaign, as well as organize neighborhoods throughout the city.

I had worked inside City Hall long enough to realize that strong community leadership was critical to any sustainable progress moving forward. So, I accepted the opportunity and challenge.

I spent the better part of the next four years forming block clubs and neighborhood associations, organizing projects and fundraisers, attending nearly every City Council meeting I could, lobbying in Columbus and the White House (yes, the White House) for policy and funding, and forming relationships with hundreds of individuals—not just from Youngstown but throughout the region and beyond.

As of the time on this writing, I'm now a small business owner in the downtown area and still working on local issues, projects, and fundraisers to help keep the forward momentum going.

---

And now 10 years have passed.

Looking back, what I have learned is that in a place of extremes like Youngstown, it's important to keep your eye on the bigger picture.

Successes and setbacks are regular, and many of them will have a real and immediate effect on the community and maybe even those you know because it's a smaller city.

People with whom you form deep relationships over time will leave for different reasons and new folks will take their place. In time, you may be one of them.

But a place like Youngstown teaches you how to balance and temper these things while still finding a way to push forward, if for no other reason than necessity.

And that's why I love Youngstown. As with many other places like it, Youngstown is a city that has a rich history, yet an uncertain future. Those who choose to help shape its future are the types of folks you probably want to know.

I have been fortunate to meet many such people over the years. That is why Youngstown will never leave me.

# THE PROFUNDITY OF YOUNGSTOWN

*By Jay Williams*

Profundity -
  1. Great intellectual insight or understanding:
  profundity of thought.
  2. Something profound or abstruse.
  3. Great extent downward; great depth.
  **4. Intensity of feeling or conviction.**

*The Free Dictionary*

F or a mid-sized city, Youngstown seems to consistently have an outsized impact on everything it touches. In victory or defeat, success or failure, exhilaration or exasperation, the city never ceases to evoke a range of emotions, reflections, or conundrums.

My entire professional career has been shaped by my life in Youngstown. It started with my first "professional" job at a local bank that was under pressure to improve its mortgage offering in the city's underserved neighborhoods, and it continues through my work today in Washington, D.C., and across the country, which more often than not, allows me to draw directly from my experiences in Youngstown.

I regularly and randomly encounter people who have a "Youngstown connection." Recently, my wife and I stopped at a garden-variety roadside fish fry in suburban Maryland, and within 10 minutes, the conversation had turned to the fact that we both had "people" in Youngstown. My daily commute on the D.C. Metro system is as likely to yield a link to my hometown as it is to endure one of its notorious "cold-weather" delays.

I have yet to envision a greater honor or a more profound experience than having been elected as both the youngest and the first African-American mayor of this city. Being from Youngstown has given me instant street cred in virtually every professional endeavor.

There are also very few cocktail conversations that don't somehow provide an opportunity to assert the relevance of Youngstown. The rise, fall and rebuilding of a local economy? Check. Hardball politics with national implications? Yep. The local food scene? Mama Mia! Sports heroes? Mancini, Tressel, Pavlik, Clarett, Pelini, Stoops. Conflicted leaders and fallen icons? Too many to mention.

Youngstown was certainly not the first post-industrial city to wrestle with the one-two punch of population loss and economic collapse. However, Youngstown was among the first cities to openly acknowledge the need to aggressively manage its decline in a way that was counterintuitive to what similarly situated cities had traditionally pursued. Youngstown adopted a mantra that smaller and different didn't have to mean inferior. The assets of the city's past industrial might could provide strong foundations to build a more diverse and sustainable future. Youngstown's talents in "making things" could be translated into a new economy.

A number of less noticed, but still critical incremental occurrences conspired in Youngstown's efforts to return to relevance. Each of those things could warrant its own chapter in the Youngstown novella. However, one pivotal point in the process occurred when the Raymond John Wean Foundation made a seismic shift in its investment philosophy. The Wean Foundation committed millions of dollars to supporting nimble, grass roots, civic-driven organizations that were taking on the most difficult challenges in the city's neighborhoods. The dividends of this investment are fueling the activity on the ground in Youngstown today.

Being involved in the Youngstown 2010 comprehensive visioning and planning initiative was inarguably a pivotal point in my then nascent career in public service. There has been a lot of legitimate debate about the success or failure of Youngstown 2010. And there is an abundance of evidence to support either side of the argument. I obviously have some very strong (and some would argue biased) opinions on the matter, but I won't go into the details here. What I will state, however, is that the city is unequivocally better off as a result of having gone through that process.

One of the most influential people in my life, outside of my parents, was my pastor, the late Bishop Norman L. Wagner. Bishop Wagner often spoke of Youngstown, not in the context of the problems and challenges the city faced, but in the potential the city possessed. He was an eternal optimist who could find the silver lining in any situation or circumstance. Without question, my perception of, and love for the city, was indelibly influenced by him. Bishop Wagner also spoke of service to others and living "on purpose." All of those things were certainly factors in my deciding to run for mayor.

The Mahoning Valley's dysfunctional and corrupt political machine at the time also served as motivation to chart a different course. There was little faith that any of the players in that system would give credence to what might be in the best interests of the city, as opposed to their own long-held political ambitions.

Being involved in the early stages of the Youngstown 2010 initiative also sealed the deal in deciding to run for mayor. The grueling process of conducting dozens of community meetings across the city helped fuel a desire to be a part of redefining Youngstown.

But there was one particular event that stands out. In December 2002, we had scheduled a community meeting at Stambaugh Auditorium, which was to serve as the unveiling of the initial Youngstown 2010 vision, the culmination of months of smaller community meetings. The event was scheduled about a week or so before Christmas (already a less than ideal time) and as fate would have it, the weather that afternoon turned cold and blustery and the snow arrived with a vengeance.

As we nervously prepared for the evening's event, I remember a prominent official sarcastically predicting that if we got a hundred people in the place we'd be lucky. As the start time approached, it seemed that prediction might have been overly generous. But the initial trickle of people slowly turned into steady stream. When the event kicked off at the prescribed time, more than 1,200 people from across the Mahoning Valley, Western Pennsylvania, and beyond had assembled to engage in the future of Youngstown. An event that was scheduled to run 90 minutes, ran for three hours; people lined the aisles to offer their take on the future of Youngstown.

As I stood on the stage with the others who help plan the event, I was awestruck with the sheer level of passion and energy that filled the auditorium. For a city that so many left for dead, there were clearly others who thought otherwise and were willing to help do something about it. That was a defining moment for me.

There were a number of struggles with Youngstown 2010, not the least of which was managing expectations. Youngstown's decline was attributable to a multitude of complex forces that smoldered over the course of decades. There existed no panacea for that condition and Youngstown 2010 was never intended to serve that purpose.

The plan did articulate certain goals and milestones, a number were achieved or remain a work in progress; others may never be realized. However, the plan was also meant to be a living document, rooted in the reality that the city would continue to be buffeted by challenges. One of the most important lessons of Youngtown 2010 was that the community could never again slip into stasis, waiting for the future, as it had done after the collapse of its defining steel industry.

I doubt if I would have ever run for mayor, let alone win the election, had I not been so inspired and invigorated by what I experienced during the time Youngstown 2010 was being conceived. Unlike what a few of my critics might have contended, I wasn't involved in the initiative to build a platform for political office. I was involved because it was exactly the type of civic movement I had stayed in Youngstown to join. I saw it as potentially one of the last and best chances to alter the trajectory of a city that I loved. And even with the significant challenges the city yet faces, no one will convince me that we didn't accomplish that objective.

If nothing else, Youngstown 2010 was a catharsis that changed the way people thought and talked about Youngstown. More importantly it changed the way many Youngstowners thought about themselves and their city.

Youngstown's story helped inform movements in places like

Detroit, Cleveland, Gary, IN, and so many other cities that had experienced the same economic headwinds and systemic decline. Youngstown's story became the fascination of similarly situated cities across the globe.

There is a new generation of activists, impresarios, entrepreneurs, and others who are molding, pushing, and shaping the city in ways thought unimaginable a short decade ago. What their final imprint will look like remains a mystery. But the fact they see the city as a place upon which they can make their mark speaks volumes to the changing perception of a place, the rumors of whose death have been greatly exaggerated.

There are many chapters yet to be written on the Youngstown saga. And there is certainly no guarantee of a fairytale ending. Yet, like the many of the boxing legends that called Youngstown home, it would be a mistake to think that this city is down for the count.

# "flower thieves and sun goddesses: these nights were meant for rooftops"

*{for Amanda and Lindsey who are always the honey,
and Courtney who gave us the words}*

Something profound is going to grow
along with all the plants that are
incessantly watered here in
Youngstown, Ohio, where our seasons
are winter, still winter, pre-road construction monsoon,
and road construction. These are
the monsoon days. Mischief drizzles
with the rain. Rain makes all the things
sprout. The sprouts bloom, are plucked and
consumed. I wait. I am one with the
universe. When you can feel the earth between
your toes, you can't help but be in love with
everything, especially the sunshine, because
eco-leather-clad toes get chilly in the rain.

When you're in love with everything you can't
help but insist on making life beautiful.
You compliment all of the egg sandwiches,
whiskey and words so that they never
stop happening. You frame your face with
stolen flowers. Show your collarbones to the world.

When the clouds take their siesta
from honeyhanding all of the sky, the girls
bare their legs for the sun and take to
the rooftops. They are forever scheming.
Precocious terrorists with mischief in their
eyes and smartphones in their hands.

They are wired. They are connected to everything.
They have the entire world under their thumbs.

If it doesn't look like they are up to anything,
it is because the something that was in
their eyes has already begun. Cupid is
no archer. These are the only love gods.
They throw all of the judging apples.

Three dollars or a kiss is often enough
to set things in motion. They watch
their city sparkle beneath them. They
are the honey. They are the queens of
May, with flowers in their hair and
beer in their chalices. They give their
words to the world. They feel it all.
Their hearts, they bleed.

It rains. But on nights like these,
who needs the stars? Even the moon is
frivolous when you wake up at five
ready to make out with the sun.
These are the monsoon days.
When the rain stops, all the flowers will dance.
Something profound is going to grow out of this.

*Cherise Benton*

# FAITH AND HOME

*By Nate Ortiz*

My family moved to Austintown when I was young, but all of my early childhood memories took place on Clinton Street on the east side. I remember thinking about how simple the neighborhood was. My grandparents lived two houses away from us, and I loved being able to freely float between both houses. Summers on Clinton Street were the best. My time was filled with playing in sprinklers in the backyard with the other kids from the neighborhood, helping my grandfather with his garden, and walking to Brown's Drug Store to get candy (preferably M&M's). Heck, I didn't even know what time was. I also never thought about what life was like anywhere else. Our neighborhood was full of older people who took pride in what they had. We looked out for each other. Even when my family moved to the suburbs, I still came back to the city for my family and church. I felt like I was home on Clinton Street, even when I lived somewhere else.

Church was the bedrock of my childhood. When I was younger, my parents (of Puerto Rican and Salvadorian descent) attended Spanish Evangelical. The new building has just been dedicated within the last year, but I still remember it being on Wilson Street next to a scrap yard. I loved being a member of a church that conducted all of its services in Spanish. I remember questioning why the church was built next to trash. A lot of the members couldn't speak English at all. Church was such a different world compared to Austintown, where I went to school. Church was like a secret club of sorts. At the time, it helped me understand the importance of culture. It was one thing to hear my parents and grandparents speaking Spanish at home, but it was so much more powerful to see a community together celebrating shared beliefs and histories. Looking back, it really helped me to be comfortable in very different environments, and I am thankful for it today. I've been blessed to be the young adult pastor at The Riot, the

BRIER
HILL
ITALIAN
FEST
←

SAINT
ANTHONY
CHURCH
& HALL
←

Youngstown and its surrounding areas are known for their many Italian heritage festivals throughout the summer. The most popular among them is the Brier Hill Festival on the north side where the best-of-the-best food trailers park and serve their unwavering festival-goers year after year.
**Whitney Tressel**

youth center of Victory Christian Center in Coitsville, for more than eight years, and I can say that my upbringing in Youngstown directly influenced my decision to want to guide others.

My connection to a faith community really shaped me, and my experience isn't that unusual. Youngstown is a religious city. It always has been. Different groups of citizens hold their own religions close and have shared them with Youngstown over the years. As early as the late 1800s, when steel mills were starting to boom, Irish, Welsh, Greek, Italian, and Eastern European immigrants brought their own religions with them. Greek Orthodox (St. John and St. Nicholas), Russian Orthodox (St. Michael), and Catholic (St. Brendan, St. Christine, and St. Casimir, just to name a few) traditions can still be seen across the city. Then another wave came with Syrians, Lebanese, and Palestinians. The influx of culture and religion led to conflict and violence at different times. New citizens wouldn't just give up their beliefs or heritage. Nor should anyone have expected them to.

In Youngstown, places of worship are supposed to be protected. That's why there was such community outrage in 2010 when Angeline Fimognari (who was 80 years old) was killed during a robbery attempt after attending mass at St. Dominic. The church, located on Lucius near Auburndale on the south side, is surrounded by vacant and boarded-up homes. Prior to the robbery gone wrong, crime had been on the rise in the area. But when elderly citizens couldn't feel safe walking out of church, even the most hardened residents were upset.

Places of worship are supposed to be safe from harm and worry. Yet it's hard for teens to leave their problems at the door. They come to The Riot seeking something—fellowship, friends, religion, or an escape, but they also come for help with their problems. My first year overseeing The Riot, I was forced to recognize how hard it can be for young adults to make good decisions and take advantage of the respite our center offers. I always had to think about how these teens were confronting major decisions in their lives—ones that could have long-lasting impacts. It didn't discourage me. In fact, it reinforced my decision to want to make a difference in the lives of our city's youth—its future.

As a pastor, I am blessed to interact with hundreds of teens from the city—some more religious than others. And they're succeeding in putting their own stamp on what church means in the 21st century. Even in my relatively short time as a pastor, I've seen an increasing number of young people wanting to take their causes outside of the four walls of the church. They don't want to just sit and talk about Biblical passages or how they should live their lives. They want to go into the community and take action. They don't want to settle for presentation; they want demonstration.

The youth of Youngstown are special to me. I've learned two things about them over my years in the city: they have much potential, and they need to be mentored. The teens are resourceful, creative, and hardworking. I deal with kids from the heart of Youngstown every week that have no choice but to grow up before they can enjoy childhood the way I did on Clinton Street. Outsiders would be shocked at what teens have to deal with. Societally, we hear about issues like teen pregnancy, bullying, and peer pressure to do drugs all the time. But it's different when a 13-year-old girl knocks on your office door wanting to discuss a family member who was murdered the night before. Or when a kid you've spent time talking to veers off path and ends up in the juvenile system for robbery. Or maybe even worse when a 15-year-old boy sits before you and says he thinks he wants to kill himself. Pastors are accustomed to helping people with their problems. But it still feels different when these kids are growing up where I grew up. I can look into their eyes and see my own childhood.

It's remarkable how these teens adapt and do what they need to do in order to keep moving forward. Mentorship is important anywhere, but especially in Youngstown. There are too many negative influences lurking in the city today, particularly in many of the neighborhoods. Kids start life off on the wrong track and are never guided back. They need to see the importance of preparing for a productive lifestyle rather than gaining street cred. They need to hear that their hometown is worthy of pride.

At Victory Christian Center, we open the doors of our building to youth weekly. It's supposed to be a safe place where they can gather with other teens, play games, and relax. While religion is involved, it's really more about the building of community. I want them to feel safe and welcome. And I love sharing with them why I love my city. Youngstown means a lot to me, and it always will. It's made me who I am. When I had a chance to buy my first home, I ended up in Struthers because of its location and how it made me think of life growing up in Clinton Ave. I work hard, and I don't quit. Youngstown's the same way. That spirit lets people born here know they can rise above tough circumstances no matter where they are. Youngstown is a place that will welcome you back even if you move away. With the culture of Youngstown probably ingrained in you, you'll feel like you never left.

# BOOM BOOM, BERNIE, AND TRESS

*By Vince Guerrieri*

**B**y the 1980s, it had become obvious—even to a child my age—that something had gone awry in Youngstown. I was born three weeks before the day they still call Black Monday, when Youngstown Sheet & Tube announced it was closing down one of its mills, the first volley in their ultimate disappearance. At one point, Sheet & Tube was the largest locally owned steel company in America, and the largest corporation in Ohio. It took Harry Truman all the way to the Supreme Court during the Korean War—and won. And by the time I started school in 1983, it was a memory.

For most of the 20th century, Youngstown was the poster child for the American dream. Immigrants could come to the city with little more than the clothes on their back, but if they had the work ethic to do it, they could carve out decent lives for themselves— and maybe their children would be able to do things they couldn't dream of doing. And they did come. Signs posted in mills offered safety warnings in multiple languages, evidence of the melting pot. By 1920, when Youngstown's population had tripled in 20 years to more than 130,000, fully 80 percent of its residents were immigrants or first-generation Americans.

But Sheet & Tube had been subsumed by the Lykes Corporation, which took as much money as it could out of the company and then closed it down. That showed people you could work hard, play by the rules—yet still lose your house and pension through no fault of your own.

The 1980s were a bleak time to be in Youngstown—a fact that was evident to me even as a boy. The mills had dragged with them a way of life. School districts closed buildings. Downtown became deserted. People left in droves. The department stores were swallowed up by national chains or closed. Hospitals cut beds.

But in an area that reveres its sports heroes, three men made it a little less bleak. In the Mahoning Valley, sports was a way up. You could work hard, sweat, save up a little money to buy a house and maybe a car (or if you were really lucky, a second car). Or you could be fortunate enough to be a good enough ballplayer that you could get a pro contract—or at the very least, be able to go to college for free while you played sports.

The three men—Boom Boom Mancini, Bernie Kosar and Jim Tressel—all had their shortcomings, but when someone's loyal to you when you're down, you have to return the favor, because those are the rules.

## BOOM BOOM MANCINI

It seems like every Italian in the Mahoning Valley knew him— and the ones who didn't know him personally had at least heard of Lenny Mancini.

Lenny was the original Boom Boom. He left the city for New York, the center of the boxing universe, and made his way to the top of the list for lightweight contenders with a knockout on Nov. 11, 1941, what was then called Armistice Day, celebrating the end of World War I. But U.S. involvement in World War II was a month away, and in January 1942, Lenny was drafted. On Nov. 11, 1944—three years to the day after he became the top contender for a championship—he was wounded by shrapnel in France and wasn't expected to live, let alone walk. But he was a fighter in more than just the squared circle.

After the war, Lenny fought again, this time as a middleweight, but he ended up returning to Youngstown. He got a job at General Fireproofing, a company that made steel office furniture, and continued to receive the good will of Youngstown residents— particularly those that were paisan—who remembered who he was, and who he could have been.

His second son, Ray, went to Cardinal Mooney, a Catholic school, and was class president and a three-sport athlete. (Ray was coached in two of those sports—football and baseball—by Ron Stoops, Sr., father of several power conference college coaches.) Ray had a scholarship to the University of Cincinnati, but he idolized his father, and wanted to be a boxer like him. He went 43-7 as an amateur before turning pro, making his debut at the Struthers Field House as "the second coming" of Boom Boom Mancini.

His ascent was meteoric. He was everything boxing was looking for in the early 1980s: personable, from a solid middle-class background—and white, which was a sign of how far people of Italian descent had come in America. When the Ku Klux Klan came to Youngstown in the 1920s, it wasn't anti-black as much as it was anti-immigrant and anti-Catholic. And Italians bore the brunt of their anger.

Ray won his first 12 fights before getting a World Boxing Council title shot at Alexis Arguello on Oct. 3, 1981. He took Arguello to the 14th round, but lost on a technical knockout. Seven months later, he knocked out Arturo Frias in the first round to win the title that had eluded his father.

Ray continued to schedule fights in the Youngstown area, in high school field houses in Struthers and Campbell, and in the Packard Music Hall, built by the family that had started the eponymous auto and electric companies. Everyone of Italian descent in Youngstown claimed him as one of their own. One of my paternal grandfather Charlie's prized possessions was a photo taken at a family wedding of him with Ray and Lenny.

His first title defense would come outdoors in Warren, at Mollenkopf Stadium, then the largest stadium in the area, in 1982. The capacity was listed at 22,000, but tickets were surprisingly easy to come by—not for lack of interest. The population had simply began to melt: The mills kept closing, and unemployment hovered around the 25 percent range. A local weatherman recorded a song called "Hang in There, Youngstown."

Still, more than 17,000 fans—including boxing mythmaker Sylvester Stallone— crowded into the stadium to watch Ray beat Ernesto España in six rounds. Ray was 24-1, and was the charismatic young fighter with a with a bubbly personality, million-dollar smile, and a great back story.

In 1982, Ray was set to defend his title again, on national television in a ring outside of Caesars Palace in Las Vegas. Ray's next opponent was unfamiliar even to most diligent boxing fans: a South Korean named Duk Koo Kim.

For 13 rounds, the two men—nearly mirror images in size and style—pummeled each other before the referee finally stopped the fight in the 14th, awarding it to Ray by knockout. Ray walked out of the ring. Kim was carried out on a stretcher, with bleeding in his brain. Despite brain surgery, he was dead four days later.

Ray was adrift, as were the fans in Youngstown who had cheered him on. The signs and cheering crowds he could count on upon his return home were gone. Boom Boom would always be one of us, but it was so unseemly to celebrate a man who had killed another in the ring. And Ray knew it. Like his father after World War II, he was never the same fighter after Duk Koo Kim. The endorsement opportunities that had been within reach dried up. Ray fought six more times before retiring in 1985. He came out of retirement for one fight in 1989 and another in 1992, but his career as a boxer was over.

## BERNIE KOSAR

I am a Browns fan because of Bernie Kosar, and goddamn me for it.

They say in a majority of households, children pick their favorite sports teams based on the loyalties of their father. My father, Chuck, was a Browns fan until Art Modell fired Paul Brown, the man who virtually invented the modern NFL, in 1963. Worse yet, Modell, a dilettante from New York City, waited until there was a newspaper strike in Cleveland to do it. Chuck followed Brown to Cincinnati and when the Bengals sprung up in 1968, he became a fan of the black and orange. He's been one ever since. It was a lateral move.

Youngstown's halfway between Cleveland and Pittsburgh, and the fan base ebbs and flows based on who's better. The Steel Curtain descended on Youngstown in the 1970s. But in the 1980s, because the Browns were better—and because a kid from Boardman was the guy who made the difference—Youngstown was squarely a Browns' town.

Bernie, who had a Brian Sipe poster in his bedroom in Boardman, was named the Associated Press High School Football Player of the Year in 1981. Only four years later, he was the starting quarterback as a rookie for the Browns.

After having to go to the University of Miami when Pitt and Ohio State wanted no part of him due to his throwing mechanics, which could diplomatically be called unorthodox, Bernie wanted to play for the Browns. And the Browns just happened to be looking for a quarterback after Bernie's childhood idol Sipe took the money and ran to the United States Football League. Bernie essentially gamed the system, turning pro in time for the supplemental draft in the summer, and the Browns traded four picks for the ability to draft him.

With Bernie under center, the Browns went to three AFC Championship Games in four years. But they were stymied in each one by the Denver Broncos and John Elway. It was like evil triumphed over good. Bernie was our boy, who wanted to stay in Northeast Ohio. Elway was a California golden boy who engineered a trade away from the team that drafted him, the Baltimore Colts. Shortly after that, the Colts made their midnight escape to Indianapolis.

The harsh lesson in Youngstown is that too often loyalty goes unrewarded. Art Modell said he loved Bernie like a son. Art Modell also had no problems standing by while Bill Belichick—who had all the personality of Paul Brown but none of the championships—cut Bernie in 1993. (In terms of betrayals by Art Modell, though, there was worse to come.) Belichick might have been right—Kosar had been running on fumes since the last AFC Championship Game in 1990—but there's a right way to do things and a wrong way. (Again, for Art Modell, there was worse to come.)

But by then, Youngstown natives didn't have to look to Cleveland—or Pittsburgh—for football greatness. They were getting it right in their backyard.

## JIM TRESSEL

On Dec. 22, 1985, a new football coach at Youngstown State University was announced. He was 33 years old, and it was his first head coaching job. Jim Tressel was an Ohio boy through and through. He was born in Mentor while his father, Lee, was the head coach at Mentor High School. Lee Tressel was an Ada native who was supposed to play for Paul Brown at Ohio State, but World War II intervened, and he went to Baldwin Wallace in Berea as part of the Navy's V-12 program. After a high school coaching career that included stops at his alma mater and Massillon, in addition to Mentor, Lee Tressel ended up at Baldwin Wallace, where his sons all played football for him.

Jim Tressel was a graduate assistant at the University of Akron, and an assistant coach at Syracuse, Miami of Ohio, and for Earle Bruce (another former Massillon High School coach) at Ohio State. He said being named head coach of Youngstown State was "a dream come true." Nobody talked like that about coming to Youngstown, especially not in 1985.

Between 1980 and 1990, the city of Youngstown lost nearly 20,000 in population. On average, that means about five people moved out of the city every day for a decade. Boom Boom and Bernie were area natives who left to find their fortune, and we knew they had to. But they made it a point to come back. Jim Tressel came to Youngstown—and made it sound like there was no place he'd rather be.

He was everywhere. He was on the sidelines at Youngstown State. For a time, he served as the school's athletic director. But he appeared at baseball card shows to sign autographs. He spoke to any group that would have him. And he started to win. More than that, he started to win with kids from the Youngstown area. The Mahoning Valley had prided itself on its football prowess, and Tressel was able to prove that it wasn't all talk.

In 1991, Youngstown State won an NCAA I-AA championship, beating Marshall in the championship game. The next year, the Penguins advanced to the title game again, but lost to the Thundering Herd. YSU won national championship games against Marshall in 1993 and Boise State in 1994. Tressel had assembled the best coaching record in Division I-AA (and Division I) by that point in the 1990s.

"He's made us special," Youngstown Mayor Pat Ungaro said at the time. As the population of the area continued to decline, Jim Tressel had made it a destination.

We knew Tressel would leave. Nobody seemed to stay in the Mahoning Valley a second longer than they had to. Plus, in modern college football, nobody successful stays at a small school. There's always a bigger, better deal coming. Tressel's name was mentioned in 1995 for one of those big-ticket vacancies, after Dennis Erickson left the University of Miami (Bernie's alma mater) for the Seattle Seahawks. Tressel took his name out of consideration for the job, and everyone in the Mahoning Valley breathed a sigh of relief.

He led YSU to another national title in 1997, beating McNeese State, but lost the national championship to Georgia Southern in 1999. Tressel's name was bandied about for Congress, but not seriously. At the time, the Valley was represented by another football hero, former Pitt quarterback Jim Traficant. There was really only one way for Tressel to leave Youngstown State and retain the love of fans and alumni, and as luck would have it, that's exactly how it played out.

In 2000, Ohio State named Tressel head coach of the Buckeyes. It was a move that was met on a state and national level with some skepticism, as fans and media collectively asked, "Who is this guy?" But everyone in the Mahoning Valley knew it was going to be a good hire.

Within two years, the Buckeyes won a national title on Tressel's watch—their first since Woody Hayes patrolled the sidelines—defeating Miami in the Fiesta Bowl. Even better for Youngstown fans was the role played in the title victory by Youngstown native Maurice Clarett. The Buckeyes played for two more national titles under Tressel, and made a record eight Bowl Championship Series game appearances. Ohio State won or tied for seven Big Ten titles, and went 9-1 against Michigan on his watch.

## THE YOUNGSTOWN ATHLETIC TRINITY TODAY

Ray Mancini went Hollywood. He was in a *Dirty Dozen* TV movie and *Iron Eagle 3*, made a few other movie appearances, and turned to producing. He can still be spotted in the Youngstown area from time to time. At one appearance, Chuck brought the photo his father took with both Boom Booms to get autographed. Ray said he remembered the wedding, and rhapsodized about the lavender double-breasted suit he wore to it. "I loved that suit." Mark Kriegel wrote a book about Boom Boom, *The Good Son*. It's been my finding that any type of national news coverage of Youngstown wades into cliché or mocks the area. Kriegel's book—in collaboration with Ray—was devoid of both, and both of them appeared in town to sign autographs. Ray would spend evenings in stores and restaurants, inscribing books and talking with the people who still loved him, 30 years later.

Ray talked about filming a reality show in Youngstown with his new wife, whom he married in 2014, 33 years after meeting her when she was a high school student and he was a young lightweight. "Let's face it," he said, "Youngstown is a reality show. I say that with all love, but it is." We can take that kind of gentle mocking from him, since he is one of us.

Bernie Kosar latched on with the Dallas Cowboys after he was cut by the Browns. He backed up Troy Aikman, and even took a few snaps in garbage time in Super Bowl XXVIII, getting the ring he had been denied in Cleveland. He ended his career backing up Dan Marino in Miami, his old college town.

He stayed in South Florida for a while. Bernie was heralded as a bright financial mind, but his investments took a beating in the economic downturn in 2008, and he went to the same fate as so many other pro athletes: he declared bankruptcy. He's back in Northern Ohio. He called preseason Browns game on television, his slurred speech belying a still-sharp football mind. He's always willing to talk about the Browns. In October 2012, he appeared at a United Way fundraiser in Marblehead, where I got a chance to talk to him during halftime of another Browns thumping, this one at the hands of the Giants.

"I've been waiting to do this interview for 25 years, since I was a kid on the west side of Youngstown," I said.

"Did you go to Chaney?" he asked. Chaney was always a regular opponent of Boardman, but the school had just dropped sports as a result of a reorganization within the Youngstown City Schools.

"I did."

"How does Chaney not have a football team anymore?"

I wanted to kiss him on the mouth: Youngstown's a place you might leave, but you never really escape.

Like too many other people who left Youngstown for bigger and better things, Jim Tressel was undone by scandal. The NCAA was investigating improprieties by players, including trading trophies and other memorabilia for tattoos. Tressel knew about the wrongdoing but didn't report it. Facing a suspension from the school and further sanctions by the NCAA, he fell on his sword, ultimately enabling Ohio State to hire Urban Meyer, another Northeast Ohio native, but not one renowned for his loyalty.

Tressel took a job as an administrator at the University of Akron, but it was jarring to see his traditional sweater vests in blue.

In 2014, the president's job at Youngstown State opened. Randy Dunn had been hired as president after an exhaustive search to replace Cynthia Anderson, who spent three years as president before departing. Dunn, who came to Youngstown State after being non-renewed at his previous university, was on the job for six months before bolting for Southern Illinois, which had the pull of home to him. Ironically, his replacement apparently felt the same pull.

A groundswell of support rose for Tressel to be the next university president. He wasn't an academic. He didn't have a doctorate. But he wasn't going to leave after six months. He probably wasn't going to leave after three years. And he wanted to be here.

In a way, it was the perfect hire. Loyalty was rewarded. Football success was rewarded. And flaws were overlooked—because in the Mahoning Valley, that's what loyalty is.

# 13 STAPLES

*By Maurice Clarett*

didn't wake up one morning as a child and decide I wanted to be the epitome of everything Youngstown. Yet, here I am. I feel like I've fulfilled every good and bad stereotype of the city: raised in the hood. Local football star. National football champion. Convicted felon. Entrepreneur. Advocate for social change. I reflect Youngstown—the city I love. I've made mistakes. More than my fair share. But I strive to be a good individual. Yet when people hear my name or meet me, I know they make assumptions. Just like with my hometown, they're quick to judge without even attempting to understand the totality of my existence.

I grew up in the 1980s on the 400 block of West Ravenswood on the south side. I've been told that it wasn't the best neighborhood. Looking back, I can see why it had that reputation. But as a kid growing up, I didn't categorize any of the violence occurring around me as particularly crazy or extreme. There were drugs. Domestic violence. Petty thefts. But it was all I knew. It was my reality. I lived my life day-to-day, like kids are supposed to. Chasing girls. Heading to the Boys & Girls Club. Pushing boundaries when I could. I didn't know how the outside world viewed my hometown. I wouldn't have understood their assumptions even if I did.

Around my block, I had about 20 friends, mostly guys. And like what tends to happen when you grow up with a small group, everyone wanted to be leader. The way to gain street cred in my neighborhood was to break rules and push boundaries. Questionable behavior was glorified. Stealing vehicles was a way to gain followers. As kids, we were never intending to cause harm or commit violence. Even though I look back now and know we were doing things that weren't right, I was willing to do what it took to have fame in my neighborhood. Unfortunately, like with most things, the more I sought fame, the more bad habits I formed and the less willing I was to avoid causing harm. My new habits had consequences.

If not for one event that occurred when I was 12 years old, no one reading this would know who I am. A group of the older guys in the neighborhood and I picked a house that we were sure had the most money and broke into it. Unfortunately, the owner happened to be home and nothing went according to plan. I ended up jumping head-first from a second-floor window and cracking my head open. By the time everything was over, I was in handcuffs and needed 13 staples to close the wound in my head. I wore the number 13 the rest of my athletic career because of what that night ultimately ended up meaning.

As a result of the break-in, I was facing a significant amount of time behind bars in the juvenile system. It was going to be my third incarceration. But a man named Roland Smith, who worked as a corrections officer in the system, promised the judge in my case that he would look after me if I was released to house arrest. Roland became my mentor. He coached high school football and made sure I was working out every day and trying to make good decisions. He saw raw football talent in me and helped me to see how that talent could mean a new reality. Most importantly, he thought it could provide a better outlet for my time. Being with positive people and taking advantage of my athletic gifts could mean a better future.

Roland is the reason I ended up at Ohio State playing for a national championship in 2003. But it wasn't enough. I had a series of ups and downs in my time there. I won a national title, but even though I was proud of being in college, I was taking classes like softball, golf, and fishing. I wasn't serious about being a student. I was more involved with women and drugs—namely alcohol, marijuana, and cocaine—than schoolwork. And it cost me. I got paranoid. I started robbing people again. All of Roland's efforts earlier in my life were forgotten. I never would have guessed that stealing around $100 and a cell phone would be the crime that forced me to confront my behavior.

When the guy I robbed chose to pursue charges, I tried to pay him off. I had money—lots of it, really. I wanted my freedom. When he didn't agree, I grabbed a bottle of vodka, a bulletproof vest, and some weapons and took off for his house. It's funny how things work out. On that night, I missed my exit while driving down the freeway. And a cop spotted me making the illegal U-turn. This all happened in 2006. A year I barely remember. It's hard to think of a day that I wasn't drunk or high. Ultimately, I ended up being sentenced to more than seven years in prison for my actions, but it could have been much worse. I'd spent my young adult life trying to gain street cred, and here I was headed to prison. Prison doesn't lead to street cred. Anything but, actually. It's a constant reminder of being caught doing something illegal. But it helped me. My suffering in prison led to my maturity. I read everything I could while serving my time. And I began to care about education in a way I never had before.

Throughout my time in the system and since my release in 2010, I've thought a lot about Youngstown. How it's more than its gangster history or steel folklore. It's a city where your word still matters and character means something. And I've carried it with me everywhere I've gone for that reason. Even when I moved to Columbus to be a Buckeye, I took friends from the city with me. They lived in the same apartment complex, and as a result, I never had to miss my hometown. The parts I knew of it had come with me. But now I want to make a difference. Roland Smith tried to put me on the right path, and it worked for a while. It's my turn to give back and help, which I have tried to do by sharing my story.

I never want people to tell their children to not grow up to be like me. It's upsetting to know the way my personal mistakes have impacted how others view me as a person, my hometown, or the university I attended. I want parents to look at me today and tell their kids to be like I am now. Each day I strive to make that easy to do. But I don't have regrets. People seem shocked when I tell them I regret nothing from my life. From the time I was a kid till today, every decision I made and action I took made sense at the time to me. They may not have been the right thing to do, but I was aware and have learned the importance of owning my behavior.

When I talk to groups about what I think kids in Youngstown

need, I always preach the importance of self-education. The Youngstown City Schools try hard to help the youth, but there is no denying the struggles they face. This generation believes success equals athletics or entertainment, and we must teach the kids of Youngstown they can be successful by building skills and developing an entrepreneurial spirit. Kids need to see opportunity. They can do more than just plan on being on the same few blocks forever, which is what my friends and I figure our life would be like when we were younger. They can use education to find equality; they can even leave the city and still love and help it from afar.

I wish I would have taken education more seriously before I was imprisoned. Had I taken it more seriously, I would have had skills and interests to leverage against my athletic prowess. According to the National Collegiate Athletic Association, less than two percent of college football players make the National Football League. Even among those who are successful, the average career lasts a little more than three years and there has been a significant uptick in declared bankruptcies within five years of retirement. Even the most successful professional athlete will be a former athlete for a far greater part of his or her life.

When my football journey at Ohio State ended abruptly, I had no other direction. I was a lousy student and football had been my structure. Without any real interest, I again started looking for ways to fill the void. Drugs and crime did that. If I'd understood how truly important education was, maybe I would have turned in a different direction. Now my goal is to give back to the community that made me who I am and supported me even when I was travelling down the wrong path. So here I stand now: football star, former criminal, boy from the hood, and most importantly, hopeful striver. Like the city I grew up in, I am too complex to be judged in broad strokes. The city and I are both working to help the world forget our past transgressions.

Every time I see a picture, uniform, or video of my playing career, I see the 13 on my chest. I remember the good times of excelling on a field like I knew I could. And I remember Roland. If not for him, my

freshman year of high school—where I opened eyes with my performance at Austintown Fitch—would have been spent in a juvenile
detention center for the crime that led to the 13 staples. He saw
something in me that I see when I look at the youth of the city today.
I hope they seize their opportunities, and I hope I can help some of
them the same way Roland helped me.

# AFTER JIMBO: TIM RYAN RESTORES YOUNGSTOWN'S DIGNITY IN CONGRESS

*By David Skolnick*

**S**urrounded by his family, some local labor leaders, leather-clad motorcyclists, and a group of young people, Tim Ryan stood outside in the cold at Niles McKinley Memorial on Feb. 19, 2002, to make the biggest announcement of his very brief career. His elected political experience was only slightly more than a year in the Ohio Senate, and his improbable victory for that seat had been the result of more luck than skill.

Yet, there he was saying he was going to run for a seat in the United States House of Representatives.

The announcement wasn't a surprise to me. Ryan, only 28 at the time, had conversations with me, as well as numerous others, about a possible run for the seat. I was polite but blunt. I told Ryan he might as well give it a shot. He wouldn't have to give up the state seat to run for Congress. I told him if he made a good showing—I never expected him to win—that he could always come back in a few years and give it another try.

After a quick trip to Columbus on the day of his announcement, Ryan was driving home when he picked up a Youngstown-area talk show on the radio. On the air, Ryan recalls, the host said the congressional announcement was "an immature move." The host "absolutely blasted me. I was getting hammered and wondering, 'Why did I do this?'"

It was an unlikely move for an unlikely politician, who ran an unlikely campaign.

Experienced politicians traditionally campaign by holding press conferences, raising money, hiring well-paid political strategists, and making deals for endorsements. Ryan had his high school guidance counselor as his press secretary. He spent time on the sidewalks at busy intersections with his young volunteers holding signs asking people to vote for him. He went door-to-door seeking support and aired quirky television and radio commercials, many during times when few were listening. But that was because the campaign had little money and airing ads at those times was less expensive.

Yet, Ryan was a young guy from the Mahoning Valley—another term for the Youngstown area that includes Mahoning, Trumbull, and Columbiana counties—who could help keep others his age in an area that has seen some of the largest population declines in the nation over the past five decades.

More than anything else, holding signs seemed to work the best. It was something Ryan learned four years earlier when he was the campaign manager for a losing state Senate candidate in New Hampshire.

"I thought someone was joking; that sounded insane, but it turned out to be our thing," Ryan said. "It was a very unconventional campaign. When we raised money, we used it to buy T-shirts with 'Ryan for Congress' on it. My volunteers would wear them while holding the signs to get my name out."

Ryan's campaign for Congress should have failed. Plenty of local politicians laughed at his candidacy, as did a number of his Democratic primary opponents. Instead, it resonated with the people of the Valley, which make up a majority of the congressional district. Ryan achieved one of the biggest Democratic primary upsets in the state's history.

After getting a bachelor's degree in political science in 1995 from Bowling Green State University—while there, Ryan was convicted in 1993 of disorderly conduct for having a fake ID while under age—Ryan went to work first as an intern and then as a congressional aide for then-U.S. Rep. James A. Traficant Jr., the Mahoning Valley's most famous (or infamous) politician.

"I caught the political bug from Jim, but I knew I needed to do something more with my life," Ryan said.

So he enrolled in law school in Concord, NH, and earned his law degree from the Franklin Pierce Law Center in 2000. He thought perhaps he'd get into international diplomacy.

While trying to find some direction, Ryan returned to the Valley and chose to run for an open state senate seat.

On the surface, it was a ridiculous idea. Two of the candidates in the race had organized campaigns, plenty of money, and supporters. However, both also had political enemies and their backers despised the other candidate. That divisiveness led Ryan to capture the very important endorsement of the Trumbull County Democrats.

"The party had to put my name on campaign literature, which was a big deal in the primary," Ryan said. "But I also had people look me in the eye and lie to me that they'd support me."

Enough people voted for Ryan, who won the primary, and in a heavily Democratic district, he easily won the general election.

To say Ryan didn't distinguish himself in the Senate would be an understatement. He was there essentially for a cup of coffee.

But he quickly figured out the political landscape. In 2001, Ryan's first year in the state senate, the Youngstown area's political clout was nonexistent.

Traficant, the region's longtime congressman—best known for his outrageous clothes and questionable character—was under criminal investigation by a federal grand jury for longstanding corruption. He was finally indicted in early 2002. That put Traficant's re-election bid as a Democrat on hold. In July 2002, Traficant was found guilty of 10 felony counts, including racketeering, bribery, obstruction of justice, and tax evasion; was expelled from the U.S. House, and spend seven years in prison.

Because of that, Democrats and Republicans in the General Assembly had an easy target as they sought to eliminate a congressional district in Ohio as a result of the state having to lose one through federal redistricting in early 2002.

That target was the Valley. The thought was no incumbents would be harmed. Congressman Ted Strickland, a Democrat who lived in southern Ohio, 300 miles from the Valley, would get Columbiana County and a lower portion of Mahoning. Congressman Thomas Sawyer, a Democrat from Akron, would receive nearly all of Trumbull County and much of Mahoning, including Youngstown.

Strickland and Sawyer immediately started campaigning hard in the Valley, which were the population centers of their districts. Many of the traditional Democratic Party leaders in the area embraced the two outsiders.

However, Sawyer had a big problem in the Valley, then a strong union area. In November 1993, at the urging of President Bill Clinton, Sawyer voted in favor of the North American Free Trade Agreement. NAFTA was seen in the Valley as the cause of its economic decline even though the closing of the steel mills in the late 1970s, longstanding corruption and crime, and the lack of political and business leadership were the real causes.

Strickland didn't face much opposition, but Sawyer had five challengers, all from the Valley. Only one of them was of any note— Anthony Latell, Jr., who'd served in the state Legislature and as a Trumbull County commissioner for decades. He was Trumbull County's state senator but had to drop down to the Ohio House because of the state's term-limits law. That was the open seat that Ryan won in 2000.

While Ryan should have been an afterthought, it became obvious that his ragtag campaign had serious momentum as he picked up some key union endorsements, and Sawyer began to take notice of the young challenger's momentum.

Sawyer tried to capitalize on something I discovered on Ryan's campaign finance reports: Ryan had borrowed $50,000 with his former high school coach as the loan's co-signer. Under federal election law, the coach was only legally permitted to give Ryan $2,000. It became the hottest story in the race. I wrote about it almost every day for nearly three weeks with Latell and then Sawyer pointing to the loan as proof of Ryan's inexperience and immaturity. The pressure finally got to Ryan, who stopped talking to me. It turns out I was correct that it was improper, and Ryan had to pay a $10,000 fine in 2004.

As the May 7, 2002, primary got closer, it became obvious it was a two-man race between Sawyer and Ryan. Sawyer did well in his home county of Summit and also easily won in nearby Portage County. Ryan did well in his home county of Trumbull. With no candidate in Mahoning County, that area was up for grabs. When the results came in, Ryan had steamrolled the competition in Mahoning County. He easily won the six-person primary with 41.3 percent of the vote. Sawyer was a distant second with 27.5 percent.

While Ryan's relationship with me as the area's main politics reporter and him as the next congressman was strained because of the articles, he gave me a big hug and made sure I stood by his side as he gave his victory speech to a crowd of supporters. We spoke the next day by phone and ironed out our differences.

In the general election, Ryan cruised to a victory over Republican political veteran Ann Womer Benjamin and an imprisoned Traficant, who ran as an independent.

When Ryan got to Washington, D.C., if anyone recognized him, it was as Traficant's replacement. The remarks weren't flattering. Traficant had been convicted of 10 felony counts by a federal court and was only the second person since the Civil War to be expelled from Congress.

"I got a lot of comments about Jim Traficant," Ryan said. "Some of the guys still kid me about it."

So what could Ryan do to restore the Youngstown-area's integrity? The Valley had a long and dark history of being a haven for organized crime and political corruption.

While he talked of restoring the area's integrity, Ryan worked just as hard to make it happen.

"People saw me working hard and were impressed," he said. "I put my head down and did the work needed to help my district. People knew exactly what happened with [Traficant], and I told them that I needed help."

Even so, they weren't just going to give it to Ryan. He had to prove himself. After the unlikely win in the 2002 Democratic primary, Ryan never again faced a tough election. Because of that, Ryan spent time traveling throughout the country campaigning for Democratic challengers, particularly in the 2006 election that saw

his party regain control of the U.S. House. Ryan was among the
first House members to throw his support behind Nancy Pelosi, San
Francisco's liberal congresswoman, for speaker of the House. The
work paid off and the reward was great.

"After we won the House, her staff asked what committee I
wanted to be on and I chose Appropriations," Ryan said.

During Traficant's congressional career, he coveted a seat on Appropriations, the most influential committee in Congress. The committee makes decisions on where federal money is spent, meaning
its members bring back a lot of it for their districts and can horse-
trade with other members of other important committees for favors.
While Traficant never even sniffed an opportunity to get on the committee, Ryan got a seat on it in just his third term.

Ryan had showed a knack for getting money for Valley projects
right away, but when he got on Appropriations, the money greatly
increased. Ryan obtained money for much-needed infrastructure work, the air base in Trumbull County, and particularly for
advanced-manufacturing projects at and near the universities in his
district—Youngstown State University, Kent State, and the University of Akron. When Republicans gained control of the House in the
2010 election, it stripped Appropriations of much of its earmark
authority, but it still remains an important committee.

During his time in Congress  he's in his seventh term—Ryan's
efforts have focused on helping to create an atmosphere in the
Youngstown area to help revitalize its once-proud manufacturing
industry while encouraging a focus on emerging high-tech fields. The
work hasn't been easy, but Ryan was instrumental in assisting with a
$1.1 billion expansion project from Vallourec Star, which makes metal
pipes for the oil and gas industry, and America Makes, a $75 million
3D additive manufacturing facility, both located in Youngstown.

While his voting record is largely liberal, he's received praise from
Republicans—including David Joyce of Russell to the north and
west, and Bill Johnson of Marietta to the south of Ryan—for working
in a bipartisan manner.

Like Traficant, Ryan is an outspoken opponent of unfair trade practices, particularly with China. Unlike Traficant, he isn't treated like a joke in Congress.

Ryan's name has been mentioned numerous times as a candidate to run for the U.S. Senate or for Ohio governor. While he's been tempted, Ryan isn't a risk-taker. He says he can accomplish more for the Youngstown area in the position he holds. Ryan remains in the U.S. House, where, in all likelihood, he can stay as long as he likes while continuing to gain seniority and work to improve the financially challenged Valley.

Fellows Riverside Gardens of Mill Creek Park keeps a particular shade tree on its grounds. It has a sheltered trunk embodying generations of wholehearted living; complete with loves gained and loves lost, happily-ever-afters and broken hearts. *Whitney Tressel*

# MAKING A CASE FOR YOUNGSTOWN

*By Will Miller*

**W**hen my wife and I first started dating, she lived in rural Georgia and had no knowledge of Youngstown. We hadn't been dating long enough to even really discuss what my hometown was like. Before the chance would present itself, she called one evening and told me she was about to watch the *City Confidential* on Youngstown. I immediately assumed it would be a stereotyped examination of the connection between the city and organized crime or the crippling impact of closed steel mills or a superficial look at the personalities that dominate the city's politics. When she told me it was subtitled "Mob Hits and Misses," I knew it was time to begin fine-tuning my rebuttal to everything she was about to learn.

A little over an hour later, she called back and I asked her to share what she had found out about my city since I knew better than to watch. She recalled the show's discussion of the mob and how it even insinuated we weren't very good at that ("What kind of hit man forgets to bring a second gun in case the first jams?"). Then she told me about the murder rate, the white flight, and the desolate economic conditions highlighted within the 60-minute episode. In short, she explained Youngstown was dead and possibly better off so.

The storyline sadly didn't surprise me. I've spent my life watching people respond to my announcing where I am from. Even though I grew up in Austintown, I have always taken pride in saying I am from Youngstown and the Mahoning Valley. Everyone has some assumption of what Youngstown represents. And I've crafted somewhat canned responses to deliver based on what I know of the person offering judgment. That night, with my now wife, I thought through the entire list.

I could have spoken to her about the city's athletic prowess and pride. From being able to watch local greats like Jeff Ryan, P.J.

Mays, Jeff Wilkins, and Mark Brungard excel and compete for championships at Youngstown State University to seeing future NBA player Mario Elie suit up with the Youngstown Pride, I grew up watching a higher level of athletic competition than outsiders could imagine. The cradle of coaching with the Stoops and Pelinis were matched only by the stable of championship-caliber boxers the area produced. Harry Arroyo, Rusty Rosenberger, Boom Boom Mancini, and Kelly Pavlik were all bright spots at different times. For an allegedly dead city, there are plenty of living legends and championship moments still present today. But she isn't into sports.

I could have talked about the giant willow trees at Fellows Riverside Garden and how from my first time visiting I had never felt safer than I did under their droopy branches. But I may have had too many first kisses and carved too many names (one twice!) into the trunk to keep her attention where I needed it to be. But, if those trees were alive, despite the efforts of so many carvers to inadvertently kill them, how could the city be dead?

As a surprise attack, I could have just admitted to my personal history with what she had witnessed. From watching the Traficant trial in Cleveland as a field trip in high school to seeing a family friend convicted of racketeering and extortion while serving as a county court judge, I'd experienced the impact of Youngstown politics firsthand. After all, nothing in the *City Confidential* episode was factually incorrect; It just wasn't defining. At least not for me or anyone else I knew that had grown up in the city.

I could have talked about the people, especially those I met while growing up in the basement of the Sojourner House, where my mother worked. For most of my middle school years, my mom was in charge of the children of domestic violence victims. Her main goal was to make them feel as at home as possible. I spent countless hours playing with these kids and befriending as many of them as I could. The stories I heard still stick with me today. They made me realize how fortunate I was in my own circumstances. I could have told her about the people in the neighborhoods I met while teaching in a summer program for a church housed in the old Jefferson School. Or the impact the murder of Jermaine Hopkins—a YSU football player I had gotten an autograph from only four days before his death—had on me. Or the influence of former YSU basketball coach Dan Peters. When I was in eighth grade, he responded to a random letter I sent him by calling me at home and coming to have lunch with me at my school the next day. But for her they would just be names.

I could have talked about steel. Whether I highlighted how important Youngstown was in World War II or touched on the family connections, industry plays a pivotal role in Youngstown's story. My grandfather helped demolish a mill in Warren he had originally wired long after he retired, which served as a sort of bookend for a physically draining career. The impact the Youngstown mills had on the Mahoning River tied directly into the image of a rusted, dead city. But the river had been cleaned and new high-tech industries had emerged to take the place of steel. So I figured why focus on an old economy? Plus, my wife had already graduated law school. Youngstown and steel couldn't be anything more than a court case to her.

I might have just attempted to overwhelm her with nostalgia. Don Guthrie and Stan Boney competing to tell me the next day's weather. The feeling of pride when Phillip Jean-Baptiste blindsided Steve McNair on ESPN on the first play of a 1994 YSU football playoff game. Watching Kelly Pavlik knock out Miguel Espino at Beeghly Center. Stories of my grandparents taking the train into the city to shop downtown. Buying a rabbit at the Canfield Fair. Watching Maureen Collins and Todd Hancock in *Joseph and the Amazing Technicolor Dreamcoat* at Powers Auditorium. Having Sam Crenshaw teach me how to dribble during Saturday YMCA basketball. Searching for snails on lily pads as a child. Getting my first hole-in-one at the par 3 course. Attending the funeral of patrolman Mike Hartzell at St. Christine's. But if I took that approach, it would have just been a disjointed memory dump since she knew nothing of the area.

So in response to her summarization of the *City Confidential*, I realized there was nothing I could tell her to give her a true glimpse of my city. Instead, I told her to figure out a weekend when she could fly to Columbus (I was working in Athens, OH, at the time), and we would take the journey ourselves. A few weeks later, we took that trip. We ate Wedgewood pizza and Handel's ice cream. We drove through Mill Creek Park and looked out at the city from Fellows Riverside Garden. We watched a Phantoms hockey game at Covelli Centre and a YSU basketball game in Beeghly. We walked around Federal Plaza and managed to see the Youngstown Connection perform. I drove her through where the old mills used to stand and through some neighborhoods with checkered pasts. I wanted her to see the spirit and grit of the city for herself. Unlike what *City Confidential* had shown, she needed to know this city is alive. And the only way to do that was to have her experience it.

As human beings, our initial assumptions are not always correct. My wife entered the city with some preconceived notions. Perhaps by luck, when we first pulled off State Route 711 onto MLK and drove toward downtown, BJ Allen was testing and caused a loud bang at just the right time, causing my wife to noticeably flinch. While loud noises make us all jolt from time to time, it was clear this was different. She reacted more strongly because she was in Youngstown. Three days later, after spending time in the city, she had a more informed view. People who know Youngstown—even for a short time—know it is alive and fighting.

Unfortunately, not all of the doubters of the city can make a pilgrimage to test their assumptions, so we are forced to rely on words to diffuse their potentially misguided views. It's important to remember that even the city's most troubling historical moments have shaped what it is today. I'm jealous of those who are there now, experiencing the revitalization downtown. They get to see the city's fight. The same fight that *City Confidential* episode highlighted when describing Paul Gains's unwillingness to be bullied or pressured into giving up the fight against organized crime. The fight for the Mahoning River to overcome decades of chemicals from the mills. The fight those willow trees wage every time someone carves another name into them. The names of the past have gotten bigger as the tree grows, just like Youngstown's past will always influence its present and future. We just need to remember to balance the old with the new as the city moves forward.

# LESSONS OF A LOST LANDSCAPE

*By Sean Posey*

Few American cities have changed as dramatically as John Young's namesake. Deindustrialization, urban renewal, white flight, suburbanization, and crime have all helped redraw Youngstown again and again over the past half-century. The tall spires of steel stacks that once encircled downtown are long gone. Nearly all of the landmarks that once defined the area—Idora Park, the downtown theaters, the uptown district, and the plethora of public swimming pools—exist now only in memory. As Youngstown's institutions vanish, the landscape of the city becomes ever harder to read; neighborhoods turn into fields; businesses become homes for wildlife and then morph into vacant lots; streets that once housed vibrant, mixed-use districts transform into urban war zones, then ruins.

The lessons of a lost landscape are scattered throughout Youngstown like the detritus of a past civilization. You can see them in every corner of the city now.

They are buried along with whole neighborhoods under express-way overpasses. Whispers of them float from the skeletal remains of shopping districts and the charred matchstick houses that pepper the crumbling inner city.

Few streets are as lost as Wilson Avenue, which runs alongside the vast wreckage of the east side. At one time an archipelago of monstrous mills lined one end of Wilson and a stretch of clubs, shot-and-a-beer bars, and working class diners ran along the other. When I walk down Wilson Avenue, I feel as if I'm being pulled back through the gnarled corridors of time. If I strain my eyes enough, it almost seems as if the Ritz Bar, the Copa Club, and the jazz joints momentarily reappear. If I concentrate long enough, I can almost make out the sounds of Youngstown's own Big Boogie D coming from a long-abandoned building as he warms up the crowd for a fresh-faced Chuck Berry in 1955. I can almost picture Mafioso Sandy Naples entering his sandwich-shop headquarters. I can still smell the sulfur from mills that are no longer there. Even your senses can betray you in a landscape of loss.

The east side was the last section of the city to be developed. With large rural-like sections, it could seem worlds away from the dense neighborhoods on the south and north sides. During the 1940s, planners foresaw Youngstown's population eventually expanding to 225,000 people or more. It was thought that growth would occur in east side neighborhoods like Scienceville, Lansdowne, and the Sharon Line. Suburbanization—and the decline of the city in general—ended that dream. Instead, the east side became a template for what was to happen to the rest of the city.

The weight of yesteryear hangs heavily on the north side as well. Almost no city in America had its upper class so concentrated in one area, as did Youngstown during its heyday. English, Dutch, and Colonial Revival homes filled the streets around Wick and Fifth avenues. Some of the most important barons of the iron and steel industries were ensconced in this cloistered section of the city.

The north side of the city today is a mix of hope and hopelessness, as the broken down mansions of former steel industry bosses become homes to young millennials or squatters. The residential section of Fifth Avenue remains largely vibrant, but the former commercial stretch has vanished. Once a place of shops and pedestrian activity, the county jail is now the centerpiece of lower Fifth.

The most obvious sources of stability now are the larger historic institutions of the lower north side: Youngstown State University, Stambaugh Auditorium, and the Butler Institute of American Art. The neighborhood gems—Wick Park and Crandall—are undergoing a renaissance of sorts: new and younger residents are moving in, a farmer's market is now open, and a community kitchen incubator operates in the area. Yet for areas outside of those zones, the future remains uncertain.

The nearby central business district's skyline remains the most recognizable part of the city, but the downtown itself is almost un-identifiable in places. The east side of Federal Street—the main artery in downtown—is essentially no more. Once it housed bars, clubs, outdoor markets, and venues like the Regent Theater. It was a more working class-oriented part of the downtown, where even street photographers made money photographing pedestrians. Only those yellowed images remain, however, for East Federal was largely destroyed to make way for a pedestrian mall during the era of urban renewal.

Those photographers are nowhere to be found today. As I wander the dusky corridors of the city, camera in hand, I see no well-dressed shoppers anxious for a keepsake from a downtown trip. Instead, the people I photograph are struggling to effect change in a city whose residents seem oblivious to their fate. Many will never even make a journey to the slowly revitalizing strip of West Federal that is emerging from the urban decay of the past forty years.

New restaurants, apartments, and a children's museum now occupy what was a dead zone on West Federal in the 1990s. Still, historical landmarks continue to disappear: the former Paramount Theatre fell to the wrecking ball in 2013, and the Kress Building is now a parking lot. Bulldozers threaten the abandoned Wells Building. If it falls, West Federal will be all the more impoverished for it, and the historical fabric of the downtown will fade ever further into oblivion.

Yet new development in the downtown does continue. The historic Wick and Stambaugh buildings are under renovation. The vacant Legal Arts Building will soon join them. In a cruel irony, many of Youngstown's neighborhoods have hit their highest levels of vacancy just as investment and new housing is reawakening the dormant downtown. Some fear, perhaps rightfully, that the central business district will become an insulated city unto itself, as the inner core neighborhoods melt back into nature.

And the return of nature is the reality for more and more of the city. Suburbanites remark on the ominous and dangerous reputation of many of Youngstown's neighborhoods, but much of the city is becoming more of a feral garden than a fearsome ghetto. Stairs leading to nowhere are now a common sight. I sometimes scale the long flights of well-sculpted concrete steps that once led to homes or businesses and that now lead to groundhog holes and densely wooded lots. One wonders what kinds of families, artists, and steel-workers once climbed these flights. Who were they and what became of them? Who were the people who fought to save their neighborhoods from onrushing blight? Only the soft sounds of birds chirping and the cold voice of the wind are left to answer.

The saga of Youngstown's changing landscape might be best encapsulated by the story of Hillman Street. One of the earliest developed corridors on what became the most populous section of the city, Hillman hummed with life.

Beset by conflict as racial tensions mounted during the 1960s, the surrounding neighborhoods emptied of white ethnics as African-Americans moved in. Places like Chicago Field went from hosting football scrimmages to serving as sites for enormous cultural gatherings like the Afrikan Cultural Weekend, which brought thousands from around the city annually to hear the likes of Amiri Baraka and the Harambee Singers.

The residents around Hillman got down with some of the finest jazz artists at the Casablanca Club on Oak Hill, and inner-city teens roller-skated the night away at nearby Reed's Arena. An unbroken string of homes and businesses stretched from up the hill all the way down to Woodland Avenue.

Today, Hillman is a long stretch of almost unbroken urban prairie. The fires of the nearby mills and of the long-ago Hillman Street riots have receded into the dusty confines of the past. Climbing into the vacant houses around Hillman, I find traces of that era everywhere: decades old funeral notices, faded diplomas still hanging from the walls, and flyers for parades through communities that no longer exist. They greet me and anyone else who cares to root through the remains of lost lives.

Only twenty years ago, I would have encountered a near war zone. The police referred to it as "Hillman Street Blues," a generation of inner city youth trying to survive an era of crack and deindustrialization around the city's most dangerous corridor.

"Come heavy or don't come at all," the motto of Youngstown in the '90s. The residue of that era remains in the vacant lots decorated with teddy bears and the sidewalk memorials for the dead. It lurks behind boarded up houses and in the eyes of the families left behind to mourn friends and family lost to the streets.

For those remaining in Youngstown, and those who come here seeking to be a part of its revitalization, the past is a problematic thing. The city's physical decay and the merciless change imposed on it by economic and social breakdown are still evident everywhere, even as demolition and time clear the landmarks associated with an era before Youngstown's decay.

Memory and history can both unite and divide places. The landscape of the steel city is as complicated as ever, even if it's as mutilated as ever. If we are to create a new landscape of hope, one that will be worth remembering, we must wrestle with the past and the legacy of conflict and collapse that produced it. We must help heal battered communities. We must confront the ghosts around us and lay them to rest. Historical landmarks like the Uptown Theater and the Foster Theater must be saved and repurposed; new landmarks must be created as a part of a community revitalization strategy that takes the whole city into account, not just the central business district. Youngstown must become more than a place where we remember what was; it must be rebuilt, re-imagined, and reborn.

A stairway leading to a production floor of a former General Fireproofing building. *Matt Campbell*

# WHERE YOU'RE FROM

*By Bob McGovern*

T his place sucks," said the voice in the back of the room.
The economics professor looked at the student and asked, "Are you from here?"

The student nodded.

The professor responded, "You know, I'm not from here, and I really don't understand why people would say that! Why don't you just *leave*?"

I don't remember how the student responded to the clearly rhetorical question, but that's honestly beside the point. That single exchange in a classroom at Youngstown State University's DeBartolo Hall has stuck with me for almost a decade. I never thought this place sucked. It was my place; it was all I knew. But sometimes it takes an outside perspective to remind us what we truly have. If all you've known is living in one place, that's one thing. But to have someone who chose to come there say how great it is—that is something entirely different.

Often it's a yearning for the past that causes us to lose sight of the present. For those of my generation, this nostalgia is for a time we never witnessed ourselves, but rather heard about from our parents or grandparents, very much romanticized and unencumbered by the more problematic parts of that past. Old photographs and postcards only show the positive parts of the story, just like a year-in-review slideshow on social media today. Not only is it a past that isn't coming back, it's a past that never quite existed—at least not completely.

The city is beyond recovering today; it's beginning to thrive. At this point, I could give lists of reasons things are great now, reasons to move here, reasons to come back. I could list scores of restaurants, bars, and other businesses that have opened in the past decade. I could even list other lists that Youngstown has appeared in, both good and bad.

But I won't do that, because this isn't fundamentally about Youngstown. This is about where you're from.

The story from my economics class could have happened at any university or college in any town in any country. The student could have said "this place sucks" or "I'm stuck here" about anywhere. And I once heard someone complain that "there's nothing to do" in Los Angeles. The quaint postcards, photographs, and newspaper clippings can be found about any town.

But when it's *your* town—whether where you're from or where you've landed—feel free to defend it. And not because of its past or in spite of it. Even if you truly believe the best days are behind, do your part to ensure they lie ahead.

Downtown, after a boxing event in 2012.
*Stephen Poullas*

# CONTRIBUTORS

**ELAINE ARVAN ANDREWS** is an assistant director of academic affairs and instructor of English at Penn State Shenango Campus in Sharon, PA. She earned her PhD in English at Ohio University. Her writing has previously appeared in *Women's Writing* and *The Spoon River Poetry Review*. She grew up in a Macedonian-American family in Youngstown. She moved away for 11 years, then returned to the area with her husband, Corey, to raise their two children, Louis and Lillian.

**NICK BAKER** is a Brooklyn, NY-based writer and rapper, originally from Youngstown. He has a healthy appreciation for punk rock, hip-hop, and prose, and he revels in any opportunity to put them all together.

**CHRISTOPHER BARZAK** is the author of the Crawford Award-winning novel *One for Sorrow*, which has been made into the major motion picture, *Jamie Marks is Dead*. His second novel, *The Love We Share Without Knowing*, was a finalist for the Nebula and James Tiptree Jr. Awards. He is also the author of two collections: *Birds and Birthdays*, and *Before and Afterlives*, which won the Shirley Jackson Award for Best Collection. Christopher grew up in rural Ohio, has lived in a southern California beach town, the capital of Michigan, and has taught English outside of Tokyo, Japan. His next novel, *Wonders of the Invisible World*, will be published by Knopf in September, 2015. Currently he teaches fiction writing in the Northeast Ohio MFA program at Youngstown State University.

**NIKKI (FELICIA) TRAUTMAN BASZYNSKI** is a proud graduate of Niles McKinley High School, Loyola University Chicago, and The Ohio State University Moritz College of Law. She lives in Columbus with her husband and two dogs and is grateful that a trip home is now just short car ride away.

Contributors

**CHERISE BENTON**'s first poem (composed at age three) was a rhyme about disliking her baby brother, who has since described her as "a bad kid poet up to no good." She has used poetry to explore her feelings ever since. Now she mostly writes recreational essays that analyze the minutiae of pop culture, and occasionally remembers to blog about the thrills of cooking, eating, and merely gazing at food. Her hobbies include rudimentary photography, interacting with food, and watching preliterate children read.

**JACK BOLKOVAC** was born in 1935 in Youngstown. The son of Croatian immigrants, Jack taught social studies and coached football and track at Wilson High School for 36 years. He retired in 1995. He and his wife, Joan, have three children. They all live in the Columbus area.

**SARAH BURNETT** has recently earned her master's degree in poetry through the Northeast Ohio Master of Fine Arts program. She hopes to teach in a college setting. She has big ideas but small ambitions.

**MATT CAMPBELL**'s work has been featured in art shows and county fairs, including a solo exhibit at Halliday's Winery on Lake Milton. He lives in Boardman with his young son and his wife, who is expecting their second child. His recent work has been shaped by his keen interest in the changing landscape of industry and how it has affected the Northeastern Ohio region. He is currently working on a project called "American Life," which strives to showcase the nostalgic pastimes of Americans, and the stories that helped create who we are today.

**DOMINIC CARUSO** is from Campbell, OH, and now lives in Akron. He works as the design, marketing, and communications coordinator for the Akron Art Museum. In his spare time, he operates 1701 Press, a small publishing company dedicated to advancing the work of mesmerizing voices in nonfiction and fiction. He feels lucky to have witnessed the spectacle of the Baby Doll Dance and looks forward to it each year.

**MAURICE CLARETT** was born and raised in Youngstown, where he played high school football at Austintown Fitch and Warren Harding before helping Ohio State win the 2002 national championship. Today, he resides outside of Columbus and is heavily involved with his local community and his hometown. He has spoken across the country in an effort to provide a strong message to children, teens, and adults.

**ALLISON DAVIS** is the author of *Poppy Seeds* (Kent State University Press, 2013), Youngstown poems at *Connotation Press*, and an interview with Pig Iron Press founder Jim Villani at *Flyover Country Review*. Her family has run a Youngstown-area motel and laundromat for more than 50 years. Her parents met at a Left End Show at the Agora Club.

**DIANE DIPIERO** has called Cleveland home for 19 years, but a piece of her heart will always remain in her native Youngstown. A writer and editor, she blogs about quirky life lessons at mamasgotapun.blogspot.com.

**ANTHONY DOMINIC** is a writer and journalist living in Columbus, where he covers art, jazz, boxing, and dining culture at *Columbus Monthly* and *Crave* magazines.

**KEITH GOTTBERG** currently lives in Richmond, VA, with his wife and their infant daughter. He graduated from Virginia Tech in 2009 and remains a diehard Hokie football fan. In 2013, he finished a master's degree in English from Virginia Commonwealth. He received an honorable discharge from the Virginia Army National Guard Infantry in 2008. He has never worked in a steel mill, but he has plied his trade as a residential carpenter.

**VINCE GUERRIERI** has spent pretty much his whole life in the Rust Belt. He's a native of the west side and a graduate of Chaney High School and Bowling Green State University. He's the author of two books and spent 15 years in newspapers. He lives with his wife and daughter in suburban Cleveland, where he's slowly trending toward respectability (and he's just as surprised by that as you are).

**ROB HUDAK** was born in Youngstown in 1973 and grew up on the north side, not far from where his grandparents were raised in Brier Hill. After graduating with a BFA in graphic design from Youngstown State University, he moved to New York City and started his career as a creative professional. He currently resides with his wife and son in New Orleans, where he works as a creative director, artist, and musician.

**ROCHELLE HURT** is the author of *The Rusted City* (White Pine, 2014). An Ohio native, she was born in Dayton and raised in Youngstown. Her work has been included in *Best New Poets 2013, Crab Orchard Review, Mid-American Review, The Kenyon Review Online*, and elsewhere.

**TOM KERRIGAN** is a retired sales executive. Born and raised in Youngstown, he wrote and directed a 10-minute play, *The Intruder*, in the inaugural Ten-Tucky Festival at The Bard's Town Theatre in Louisville, KY. He is currently writing a novel.

**PHIL KIDD** is an organizer, writer, and small-business owner in Youngstown. He was born in the Pittsburgh area and moved to Youngstown to attend Youngstown State University in the late 1990s. Upon returning to the area more than 10 years ago, he founded Defend Youngstown and Youngstown Nation, an effort to link independent journalism, community activism, and merchandise to advance community development in Youngstown.

**MONICA LOTT**, an Orangeville, OH, native, earned a BA/MA in English and a BS in natural sciences-biology from The University of Akron and a PhD in literature from Kent State University. Her academic writing focuses on detective fiction and examines themes of war, gender, and shell shock. She is currently an adjunct faculty member at Kent State University.

**CHRISTINE MCBURNEY** is a theater artist, educator, freelance writer, and co-artistic director of Mamaí Theatre Company. For the past 13 years, she has taught playwriting, film, acting, and theater management at Shaker Heights High School's nationally recognized Theatre Arts Department, serving for eight years as chair. She has written for *Belt, Fresh Water Cleveland, In Theatre* magazine, *The Plain Dealer, CWRU Magazine, Northern Ohio Live*, and others. She lives in Cleveland Heights with her cat, Django, and her son, Ciarán, when he is home from The Ohio State University. She is a proud graduate of Struthers High School, class of 1983.

**BOB MCGOVERN**, a Mahoning Valley native and lifelong northeastern Ohioan, is a Youngstown State University-educated economic analyst with a background in political science, music, and economics. While he is enthusiastic about a number of subjects ranging from cooking and coffee to language and travel, he particularly takes an active interest in his home of Youngstown and the Mahoning Valley, as well as in their future. He currently sits on the board of the Mahoning Valley Young Professionals and is the co-organizer of TEDxYoungstown.

**MARK MORETTI** has been an editor, reporter, and photographer for newspapers and now works in the communication field. He was raised in Hubbard and lives with his family in central Ohio.

**ERIC MURPHY** is a documentarian, writer, director, and producer with more than 25 credits to his name. Notable works include the award winning short film *Steel Valley* starring *Modern Family's* Ed O'Neill and writing/producing credits on the History Channel series *Ancient Aliens and America's Book of Secrets*, as well as writing credits on the upcoming series *The Civil War in Color*. Previous editing work includes national commercials and documentaries for Warner Bros. and The Academy of Motion Picture Arts and Sciences. Murphy developed his fascination with politics during his tenure as director of communications during the Ohio Senate campaign for current U.S. Congressman Tim Ryan. Born and raised in Warren, OH, Murphy grew up listening to local legends about mobsters and "crooked" politicians. A proud alumnus of Youngstown State University, Murphy earned a BSBA in Film Marketing and proceeded to earn a MFA in Film Directing from Loyola Marymount University in Los Angeles.

**GORDON MURRAY** was born in Youngstown, OH, and is a professor at Kent State University.

**ED O'NEILL** is best known for his role as the main character, Al Bundy, on the FOX Network's long running sitcom, *Married... with Children*, and most recently for his role of Jay in ABC's hit series, *Modern Family*. Born in Youngstown, O'Neill attended Ursuline High School. He attended Ohio University and Youngstown State University, was signed by the Pittsburgh Steelers (cut in training camp) and was a social studies teacher before becoming an actor. He has appeared in several movies, including David Mamet's *The Spanish Prisoner* and *Spartan, The Bone Collector, Little Giants, Dutch*, and the *Wayne's World* series. O'Neill has had notable television roles including Sgt. Joe Friday on Dick Wolf's remake of *Dragnet* and a recurring role as Baker on NBC's *The West Wing*. He also played Detective Michael Mooney on David Milch's *Big Apple* and a retired cop on the HBO series *John from Cincinnati*.

**NATE ORTIZ** was born and raised in the Youngstown area. He currently is the director of the youth center at Victory Christian Center where he has served for the past nine years. Nate, his wife, Lisa, and son, Amari, are proud to call Youngstown home.

**LEAH PERRINO** is a graphic designer and photographer working in Los

Angeles. She grew up in Youngstown and graduated from Kent State University with a degree in visual journalism with a concentration in information design.

**SEAN POSEY** is a multifaceted photographer, writer, and historian. He holds a degree in photojournalism from the Academy of Art University in San Francisco and a master's degree in history from Youngstown State University. Sean is the urban affairs chair at the Hampton Institute and is currently working on a book about Youngstown for the History Press, which will be released in early 2016.

**STEPHEN POULLAS** is a Youngstown-born-and-raised photographer who resides with his family on the city's south side and enjoys documenting the city's evolution.

**MIKE RAY** is a west side native who has represented the Fourth Ward on Youngstown City Council since December 2010, and he is an active participant in west side neighborhood associations. He is a graduate of Chaney High School and Youngstown State University and remains active in the Youngstown community as a trustee for a local foundation and as a board member on two nonprofit organizations. Mike works as the marketing/customer service coordinator for a Pittsburgh-area company that provides environmental testing services for electric utilities.

**SARAH SEPANEK** is a Mahoning Valley native, proud Youngstown State University alum, journalist, editor, and former columnist with the Warren *Tribune Chronicle*. She recently moved to Texas, but don't worry, Ohio. She'll be back.

**NICHOLAS SERRA** is a software developer and photographer living in Youngstown.

**DAVID SKOLNICK** has written for *The Vindicator* in Youngstown since

May 1995. In September 2000, he was named the newspaper's politics writer. A newspaper reporter since 1988, he has interviewed dozens of elected officeholders and presidential and vice presidential candidates and broken many national news stories. Skolnick has won numerous awards from the Associated Press, the Ohio Society of Professional Journalists, and the New York State Newspaper Publishers Association. He has appeared on several national networks including C-SPAN, CNN, MSNBC and Fox News, as well as on NPR and on radio stations throughout the country, and in numerous websites, newspapers and magazines. He resides in Austintown with his wife, Elise, and his daughters, Spencer and Logan.

**SARAH STANKORB** is a freelance writer and regular contributor to *GOOD Magazine.* Her articles and essays have appeared in publications including *The New York Times, TheAtlantic.com, Slate, Salon,* and *CNNMoney.*

**STAN K. SUJKA** is a physician, writer, and poet. His writing has appeared in the *Orlando Sentinel, Chicken Soup for the Teacher's Soul, Mace Magazine, Florida Physician,* and a number of academic medical journals. Currently, he is practicing urology in Orlando. Dr. Sujka is a graduate of Poland High School (1974) and Youngstown State University (1978).

**LORI TAMBURRO** is a native of New Springfield, OH. She graduated from Youngstown State University and works remotely as a technical writer for a software company in Solon, OH. She currently resides in Santa Fe, NM, with her husband, Sam, and her cat, Tito.

**C LEE TRESSEL** grew up in Youngstown and its suburbs. After brief stays in Chicago, Minneapolis-St. Paul, and Berea, OH, she now lives in rural Indiana where she reads, writes, and grows grain with her farmer husband. She posts the occasional essay at cleetressel.com.

**WHITNEY TRESSEL** is a photographer and photo editor based in New York City. After spending the first 18 years of her life in Youngstown, she proudly and frequently returns for ongoing projects and commissions. Since moving to Manhattan, Whitney has worked for a range of magazines, including *Rolling Stone, Esquire, Hemispheres,* and *Budget Travel,* where she photographs, art directs, and produces photo shoots domestically and internationally. Each summer, Whitney teaches photography to high schoolers through a *National Geographic* program, so far covering Barcelona, Paris, and Costa Rica.

**DAWN WEBER** is a national award-winning humor columnist, author, and blogger. Her work has been published in four books, and she's just finished writing her own full book of essays. She blogs at http://lightenupweber.blogspot.com, and writes the "Lighten Up!" newspaper column in the *Buckeye Lake (Ohio) Beacon*, for which she won a 2011 National Society of Newspaper Columnists humor award. She resides in Brownsville, OH, (motto: Indoor Plumbing Optional) with her family and an ever-changing series of dirty, ill-mannered pets. Her goals include thinner thighs, a nap, maybe a solo trip to Target.

**JAY WILLIAMS** was appointed by President Obama to serve as the assistant secretary of commerce for economic development and was sworn into office on May 20, 2014. As the administrator of the U.S. Department of Commerce's Economic Development Administration (EDA), Williams is charged with leading the federal economic development agenda by promoting innovation and competitiveness, preparing American regions for growth and success in the global economy. Prior to joining the Department of Commerce, Jay served as the executive director of the Office of Recovery for Auto Communities and Workers. He also served in the White House as deputy director for the White House Office of Intergovernmental Affairs. Williams served as the mayor of Youngstown from 2006 to August 1, 2011. Assistant Secretary Williams was born and raised in Youngstown. He graduated from Youngstown State University with a BSBA, majoring in finance.

**ANDREA WOOD** was born and raised in Pittsburgh. A graduate of Penn State University with a degree in political science, she was hired in 1974 as the first woman newscaster at WYTV Channel 33. She worked at television stations in South Bend, IN., and Pittsburgh before returning to WYTV in November 1979. Today she is the president of the Youngstown Publishing Co. and publisher of *The Business Journal*. She resides in Poland, OH, with her husband, Dennis LaRue.

**TOM WOOD** is a writer, mountain rescuer, and industrial rope rescue trainer. A 1990 graduate of Kent State University's photojournalism program, he is also a former combat photographer for the United States Marine Corps Reserve. He's written articles and presented webinars on rescue-related topics for both print and online magazines, such as the *Meridian, Colorado Serenity, Advanced Rescue Technology, Firehouse World* and is a contributing editor for the rescue textbook *High Angle Rope Rescue Techniques: 4th Edition* (2014), Jones and Bartlett. He lives at an elevation of 8,400 feet in the Colorado foothills west of Denver in a house that is much too small for a family of five with two cats.

# ACKNOWLEDGEMENTS

We thank the contributors, especially Sean Posey for the arresting cover photograph and Phil Kidd and Christopher Barzak, who helped us make connections. We are grateful to Leah Perrino for designing this book so beautifully and to Zoe Gould for her skillful wordsmithing. Much thanks goes to Anne Trubek, too, for her vision and guidance. Her company, Belt Publishing, has amplified local voices in Rust Belt cities like Youngstown. We are proud to join Cleveland, Detroit, and Cincinnati in the fulfillment of that mission. And a special thanks to Jim Babcock, who even from the outside, saw that Youngstown has a special story to tell and made this book possible.

# ABOUT THE EDITORS

**JACQUELINE MARINO** is an associate professor of journalism at Kent State University. Her essays and articles have appeared in many publications, including *Cleveland Magazine, The Plain Dealer, The Christian Science Monitor* and *River Teeth: A Journal of Nonfiction Narrative.* She is the author of *White Coats: Three Journeys Through an American Medical School* (Kent State University Press, 2012). A graduate of Cardinal Mooney High School, she grew up in Boardman.

**WILL MILLER** is director of institutional research and effectiveness at Flagler College, where he also teaches in political science and public administration. His essays and articles have largely been published in academic journals prior to this endeavor. He is the author of *Tea Party Effects on 2010 U.S. Elections, The Political Battle over Congressional Redistricting, The 2012 Nomination and the Future of the Republican Party, Taking Sides: Clashing Views on Political Issues* (19th ed.,), and *Campaign Craft* (4th ed.) He graduated from Austintown Fitch.

# ABOUT BELT MAGAZINE

*www.beltmag.com*

"Marking its first year in publication, Belt Magazine, with its focus on the industrial Midwest, is the nation's new literary darling."

*- American Prospect*

"Belt Magazine, a Cleveland-based, online publication focused on life in the Rust Belt, practices principles that ring almost quaint in the new media age. It assigns editors to work with writers on long stories with original reporting, writers who in turn get paid for their work. The result is a selection of stories and essays that often offer fresh insight into regional issues and challenges and that stoke smart conversation."

*– Cleveland Plain Dealer*

"It's the sort of writing you won't find anywhere else, both in scope and talent."

*– Cleveland Scene*